You ARE the List

for Adrienne

Jean

Soul Adventures

Jean Adrienne

With
Mardeene B. Mitchell

Soul Adventures
By Jean Adrienne
With Mardeene Mitchell
Published By:
InnerSpeak Publishing
690 Wexford Hollow Run
Roswell, GA 30075

Editor: Maureen Alvord
Cover Art and Design: Deborah Hill, Online Creative, Inc.
Author's Photograph by Mardeene

ISBN, print edition 0–9728026–6–5
Library of Congress Control Number 2003101723
First Printing 2003
Printed in the United States of America

Soul Adventures   *Jean Adrienne*

I AM the soul
I AM the light divine
I AM love
I AM will
I AM fixed design

Alice B. Bailey
Channeled from Djwhal Khul

Table of Contents

Acknowledgements

This book would not have been possible without the help of wonderful friends and teachers. I would like to thank Patricia Squires for opening my eyes to the idea that I could write and Mardeene Mitchell for coaching me to higher levels in this effort. I also wish to thank Lisa Yoho, Jill Gray, and Patricia Squires for their painstaking proofing work. I am also most grateful to Deborah Hill for her beautiful artwork, cover design and advice. But, most importantly, Larry, for being so patient and supportive through this entire process – "Thanks and I love you!"

Prologue

"You need to meet this woman, I don't know why, but I'm supposed to give you her card." I was intrigued. In February of 2001, one of my clients handed me the business card of this mystery woman I was supposed to see. Immediately my ego–centered mind went to work. I thought she could potentially be a new student for my work, the InnerSpeak Process. The card listed five modalities the woman herself practiced: Reiki, Karuna Ki, Life Coaching, Seven Rays Healing and DNA Activation. Silly me! I scheduled one of her DNA activations thinking that I could meet her through that and besides, "I've wasted $50 on worse!" When Patricia Squires appeared at my door, I knew I had been mistaken. She had a lot to teach me, not the other way around!

There are no words to describe exactly what took place during this process. On the surface it was a meditation, but I'd never experienced a meditation where I "saw" such beautiful colors and felt such peace. At no time did she touch me physically, but I "felt" her open my crown chakra and come inside my head, working with my physical DNA. I know I did not want the meditation to end!

At the conclusion of this extremely powerful experience, Patricia said, "Oh, by the way, they tell me you are about to write a book." I responded, "No, I don't write, I only make to–do lists and bulleted sales presentations, nothing more!" Boy, was I wrong. My creativity was opened by that activation, perhaps for the first time in this lifetime, and my book began flowing out from it. A great deal of personal healing has happened to me during this writing, and I thank Pat for getting me started.

We are moving through a period of rapid growth and consciousness–raising, both as a species and as a planet. We are learning more about ourselves with each passing day. Every incident in our lives is both a lesson and a blessing, and becomes even more so based on how we react to it emotionally, physically and spiritually. As I have explored my life, as well as all the lives of my soul that I've been able to connect to, I've been able to learn so much from these little dramas. My wish is that as you read my story, you will find areas that will help you as well to remember who you really are.

Jean Adrienne, Roswell, GA

Part I
The Mission

Chapter One
The Chambered Nautilus

I saw a picture in a magazine that caught my eye. It was a drawing of a chambered nautilus. "If I ever need a logo for anything, this is what I want," I mused. The drawing was clipped out and stuck in a folder in my desk. When I decided to start healing work, I needed a business card, so the drawing was pulled out, scanned in and became my logo. Why it should represent the work I do was never considered, it was pretty and I responded to it. About a month after I had the DNA activation, I attended a workshop on Seven Rays healing that was taught by Patricia, who was now my new teacher and my friend, as well as Massimo, her significant other and fellow Seven Rays Master. Seven Rays is a channeled healing modality that uses the influence of the Ascended Masters to facilitate powerful healing changes. It was a two–day class, Saturday and Sunday, and introduced me to a lot of new material. I was exhausted when we left Saturday night, and went to bed almost immediately after I got home.

About 2 a.m., I awoke, startled, hearing, "Please put the soles of your feet together. Please put the palms of your hands together." It was a man's voice, quite loud. I looked over to see if it had awakened my husband, but he was snoring away, oblivious. So, I did as I was told. I guess I fell back to sleep, but maybe I was half awake. What happened next was even more interesting. On the screen of my mind, I began seeing images. It was like viewing a Powerpoint presentation. The images were drawn in violet ink on a violet background and they were blueprints – buildings, flowers, bugs, bodies, seashells and machines. They flashed quickly, too quickly for me to focus on them individually. Bizarre!

The next morning, I got to class early. "Pat, you won't believe what happened to me last night," I shared excitedly. After she heard my story, she went running to another room and brought back a book, *The Ancient Secrets of the Flower of Life* by Drunvalo Melchizadek. She flipped through it and handed me the open volume. "Is this what you saw?" she asked. Imagine my amazement! She was showing me EXACTLY what I had seen the night before. The blueprints in this book were all examples of Sacred Geometry and the fibronacci spiral, the formula that is the basis for all living things! Spirit had done a "download" of Sacred Geometry into me during the night! Here's the kicker – the chambered nautilus is one of nature's finest examples of the fibronacci spiral.

As my work, InnerSpeak, began to be channeled in to me, the first information I received from Spirit was that this new work was to be based on Sacred Geometry. It was to be based on 3 squared or the number nine, the number of the Christ Consciousness according to *The Flower of Life* material. Next I was told that I would have 144 files, another significant number in Sacred Geometry. And then the files began to flow in. For the next three months, basically all I did was write. The InnerSpeak manual is based on the number nine and is 210 pages, 144 files, several of which have been included in the appendix of this book as examples of what came in. The InnerSpeak process works at a deep level to promote clearing, healing and the raising of consciousness. It allows one to get to the root of old karmic contracts and examine them in the context of what occurred. Once the complete picture of what happened is clear in

4

relation to all those that were involved at the time, forgiveness of all players can take place and the contract can be brought to a closure, once and for all. The 144 files contain snippets of information that can be connected together to weave a story. By using kinesiology, or muscle testing, InnerSpeak provides a language for the client's sub-conscious mind to use. We will examine it in more detail later.

Chapter Two
The Work

Since my awakening that began with the DNA activation, I have been able to focus more clearly on why I'm here doing this work. I've gained a better understanding of what my life is all about, what my mission really is in the grand scheme of things. While the surface glance shows that I am doing emotional, spiritual and physical healing, the truth is that my work is all about helping the people lying on my table to reclaim their power. In every case, the basic element that needs to be healed for a person is fear, and the cure is personal empowerment.

How we reach this conclusion is different for everyone, and certainly how we heal it is as well. But, each healing session has basically the same format. I ask the client what is up for them, what they want to work on. Many times the person is real clear about what's not working in their life, but sometimes they have no clue. They just know they aren't happy and things aren't flowing in the way they would like. Or, they know they are supposed to be here for a purpose, but they just can't seem to find what that purpose is. So they come to me to find what is keeping them stuck, or held in a place of "no change," to bring it up for examination, and facilitate its release.

The primary cause of unhappiness or illness is the belief that one is separate – from God and mankind. This belief in separation is what then translates into fear. The goal, then, is to remove anything that causes one to feel separate. When the force that is blocking progress is cleared from the client, it is removed from the ancestor or past life existence that set it up, as well. Since quantum physics has shown that time is nonlinear, this can happen in an instant during the session, and the cycle of fear can be ended. These forces display signals from our Inner, our very own soul that something needs to be attended to or looked at. Since the Inner constitutes the blueprint of our existence, then all our pains, our health, our dreams, our appearance, our feelings, the events and circumstances we undergo, our hopes and our fears – all are signals, displaying our blueprint's condition. These signals can include physical problems, unwanted, inappropriate or uncontrollable feelings, destructive actions and impulses, inappropriate beliefs, unwanted identities we have taken on as our own, and spiritual disconnection and loss of faith.

Four things are required for any healing to take place. First, one must give their permission. Second, there must be conscious involvement on the part of the person to receive the healing. Next, the healing must take place at the level of consciousness and within the belief system of the client, and last, it is gratitude that owns the healing. I use a form of clinical kinesiology, combining muscle testing and hand positions to enable the soul or Inner to communicate where traumas and forces exist. Muscle testing is a modality that was originated by Dr. Charles Goodhart over forty years ago. Dr. Goodhart found that he could isolate a muscle or group of muscles and that by testing the relative strength or weakness of that muscle or group, he could gain information about the health of the body. Many have built on his work over the years. Clinical kinesiology, developed by Dr. Alan Beardall in the seventies, added hand positions or mudras to take the work to a deeper level and gain even more information from the body. This work runs through a series of files and the muscle testing is used to select which files and what information in those files the inner wants to use to describe what's going on in the life of the client. Some of the information that is received is the source, or root cause, of the blockage, what happened that set the force up, where and when, and what the client needs to do to remove the block and end whatever karmic contract might be in place. This background of healing work and study led me to the creation of a healing modality of my own, InnerSpeak, allowing me to help others to heal and begin their individual tasks of taking responsibility for co–creating their own reality, dismissing any thoughts of being a victim. InnerSpeak sessions are conducted in surrender to Spirit. I merely facilitate for the clients by listening to what their Inner has to say and communicate that information back to them in a way that they can understand.

We first look for the source of the force that the client is dealing with. This is generally something that happened to their soul in either the present incarnation, something that happened in a past life, or something traumatic that happened to an ancestor. Next we locate the cause, the traumatic event that started the chain reaction we are dealing with in the session.

Then we look at the reaction of the soul to what occurred. InnerSpeak differentiates itself from more traditional therapy because with this process, not only are the forces causing problems brought up for examination, but the Inner also communicates what is necessary to allow the force to be released and the associated karmic contracts to be completed. This modality is very specific in telling what the client needs to do to facilitate removal of a force.   I call this facilitation part of the session Renewal, because it involves not only clearing away the force, but also replacing it with something positive. This is done through a series of therapies. Some examples of therapies include visualization, prayer, aromatherapy, Bach flower remedies, acupuncture, crystal, sound and color therapy, and much more. The client often comes in, feeling like an emotional "basket case," and after completing a session leaves feeling clearer and lighter, since all the "stuff" that has come up during the hour has been lifted off. Empowerment occurs because the client is the one creating the healing. I provide a safe space for this to occur, and I give them the necessary information from their Inner to do what is required, but they do the work. It's hard work, but gentle, non–intrusive. And, finally, together we give thanks to God for assisting us with the healing. Many times, the actual energy shift doesn't take place until this occurs.

Unlike most energy work that I've experienced, there are no painful side effects and the processing is generally easy. There are occasional tears of release that come quickly and then are gone. People come to me, stuck or in fear or ready to move out of fear, saying things like "I keep losing jobs," "I'm having financial problems," or "Men/women keep leaving me." In most cases, one session can clear up a particular issue. This doesn't mean that a client only needs one session, though. We've all had many lifetimes and created many forces, so most of my clients decide for themselves that they want additional sessions to work on the things that come up in day–to–day life that block their forward progress. My goal, then, is to clear whatever is blocking the client from every lifetime where it's been an issue, as rapidly as possible, so they don't have to keep struggling with the same thing over and over. I used to focus on one lifetime or one issue per session, but now my work and my results are expanding with amazing results! I realized you can ask God for $1 or you can ask God for $1,000, and the answer will still be YES!

I wasn't asking for enough. Now I ask that this person's issue be cleared for every lifetime in which it has been a problem. Not only that, I ask that everything be cleared from all lifetimes we deal with in that session – and cleared as well for all other souls involved! It's working. For example, one client may have been betrayed by his spouse in 15 lifetimes, and now we clear all of them of not only spousal betrayal, but also of other debilitating issues that have been carried forward through many lives. When people ask how often they need to see me, I respond, "You'll know when you need another session!"

Chapter Three
Client Successes

Patricia's Story

What Patricia had to say now, some nine months after we first started working together, was all new information to me. I didn't find out about this until I started interviewing clients for this book. It turns out that when I contacted Patricia for the DNA activation that started this whole process off, she was in the middle of a major life crisis. Unbeknownst to me, she and Massimo, her partner, had broken up just before I met her. The first session I did on her was a trade. She was going to work on me with the forms of energy work she used, and I would give her an InnerSpeak session in return.

"So, Pat," I asked. "What would you like to work on today?" She answered, "Well, I don't have anything in particular that's up for me right now, so why don't we just ask Spirit what needs to be looked at?" That's my favorite answer, because regardless what the client thinks is their big problem, their Inner will prioritize and will present the most important issue for examination. Surrendering to Spirit to make the choice just makes things easier for all concerned!

Her session was about a past life and her relationship with an angry warrior. The force she was running was a culturally implanted taboo – she was not allowed to leave the relationship. A prohibition placed on her by her tribe held her trapped in an abusive situation. When she cleared the karma from that lifetime and ended the contract, she also cleared her relationship with the reincarnation of the warrior's soul, Massimo.

Massi was born angry. Pat had been struggling with guilt throughout their relationship, feeling like she owed him for some reason – a reason she didn't know or understand. These guilt feelings were keeping her from leaving, but not for the right reason. They had broken up out of anger, and she'd left out of anger and fear. Her session was on a Thursday. She had to process what had come up in the session for three days. The next time she spoke to Massi was Monday, concerning a meeting they had previously arranged for Tuesday. Both of them were surprised at the shift in energy. Neither expected a resolution, because the meeting was concerning a joint business venture, but at the conclusion, dialog had begun and within a few weeks he moved back in and their relationship has healed.

In the year that has passed, they have had their ups and downs, but no longer are they bound together by fear or by tribal rules that are hundreds of years old. Both Patricia and Massimo continue to work with me when one or the other feels an issue surface.

Linda's Story

I met Linda at a lead–sharing group I joined to boost my healing business and attract more clients. Most of the people in this organization were from traditional jobs– real estate, mortgage brokers, investment brokers and the like. As you might imagine, when I introduced myself and told about my work, they looked at me as if I had three heads! Even though I felt like leaving, something told me to join and persevere. Within several months, almost the entire group had come to me for at least one session, just out of curiosity. Two of the women came for more than one session – one of them was Linda.

Over the years of doing healing work, I've learned several things: First, don't have any attachment to the outcome of the session. Make no promises and work in complete surrender to God. Second, don't judge the session by how it appears on the surface. Some of the most profound healing has occurred in sessions that I felt were quite blah, and some of the sessions I thought were the most powerful have had little or no apparent impact on the client.

Linda's first session was one of the former (probably because I was wanting it to be really profound). She was dealing with a Qi state, an energy blockage, that would come up for her every time she tried to make any meaningful change in her life, such as increasing her business and enhancing her income, deepening family ties, or the "biggie", figuring out why she is here and what she is really supposed to be doing this lifetime. Ii is energy that flows through our bodies in river–like meridians, just under the skin, according to traditional Chinese medicine. These meridians are similar to our circulatory system, but would never show up in an autopsy– they are strictly energetic. When these meridians are blocked, and energy can't flow smoothly through them, we begin to experience dysfunction and dis–ease. In her first session, Linda came to me wanting to work on losing weight, so we jointly surrendered to Spirit and asked for help in looking at what needed to be looked at for Linda's highest and best good to remove anything that was blocking her from that goal.

What I found was that the acupuncture point that was blocked was kidney 17, which is all about holding onto a belief that one is complete, when, in fact, there are areas of frailty that need to be corrected in one's life. This belief was causing her to hold on to status quo, keeping her weight from dropping regardless of what she tried.

"Linda, I'm getting that this belief was a force you took on when you descended into incarnation, but it's a force that was set up in your deep ancestry, over 20 generations back. This ancestor was a Native American." Linda did several visualizations, but the surprising thing for both of us was that this ancestor was "right there" for her, waiting for release. She'd never done this type of energy work before and didn't realize that she was capable of finding and healing a long deceased relative! She quickly found this man, a shaman, and allowed him to show her what happened to him in his lifetime that caused him to operate from his ego–self rather than his higher self.

As a facilitation, she was asked to find that ancestor's totem animal, become that animal and heal it from within. Totem animals are a very important part of Native American spiritual cosmology. They represent the "medicine," the person's talents, gifts, and abilities as well as their challenges, which a person carries in their walk on this earth. The totem animal that was there for Linda's ancestor was the wild boar, which is about confrontation according to Native American folklore. The lesson for the ancestor and for Linda was that it was time to confront everything and everybody that each had avoided thus far. While this was an important lesson, no doubt, in my mind it didn't qualify as "profound." I just figured that would be the last time she'd come for an appointment because nothing really happened. She left smiling and thanked me, and I figured that we'd see each other from time to time at the referral group.

I was amazed when she contacted me later and told me that the session had changed her life! She began to come on a regular basis and we worked on lifetime after lifetime, opening her to many spiritual gifts. It's important to note that over the last year that we have been working together, Linda achieved her goal. In addition to clearing issues around confrontation, she has also lost over fifty pounds!

She began to realize over several sessions that she is quite psychic and has the ability to see the spirits of those that have crossed over. It seems that she'd always had this gift, as she'd seen images of people and things before, but just didn't understand what they were and had dismissed it as her imagination.

One session was about a past life in the Boston area several hundred years ago. In that life, she was a woman who had psychic abilities, but was stifled by her family and written off as "crazy." In order to clear the force, she was to visualize this woman that was her and tell her that she was ok. Most of the time, when clients are doing visualizations, I leave the room, to remove as much of my energy from their field as possible so that I don't interfere. When I knew she was done, I went back in. Linda said, "Well, she was here– no, I mean really HERE! She liked the music and she stayed here with me and danced for a long time!" This was confirmation to us both that she could see those that were on the other side. As time went on, her gifts deepened. One day in session she asked me, "Who is the "guy" who's standing on my left, next to the table?" I closed my eyes and asked my own guides and got that it was one of the Ascended Masters, Kuthumi. She said, "cool!" stood up, paid me and left. About an hour later, she called me, quite upset. She said, "That guy won't leave me alone. He's been with me in the car all the way home. He insists that I call you. He can't understand why I didn't ask you what he wanted when I asked who he was. He said you'd know!"

I was blown away. Not only did I not know, I had no idea how to find out! I didn't want to admit that, so I told Linda I'd meditate and try to get an answer for her. When I relaxed and asked, good ol' Kuthumi was right there chuckling away. I asked him why he'd appeared for Linda and he said, "I am ready to work with her, to teach her." Then he said, "I'm ready to work with you, too. All of us have been trying to work with you and teach you, but you won't listen! Every time you think you are meditating, we can't cut through your inner noise. You are either, humming, singing or chatting non–stop! The only way we can get you to listen is when you are listening for one of your clients, so that's why I made Linda call you." Our angels and teachers have such a great sense of humor!

The most recent session I did for Linda was even more profound for me than for her. In a past life of hers in France, around the first or second century, I found that we were twin sisters, inseparable we thought. We went everywhere and did everything together.

For some reason in our early teens, the "powers that be" chose to separate us. This was for cultural, religious or group reasons, but we weren't told why. We were separated for the remainder of our lives and neither of us ever knew what happened to the other. As this began to emerge in the session, I was overwhelmed with grief, long–standing grief that I've held within throughout this life as surely as I have for all others.

I began to sob and was almost unable to finish the session. Linda, on the other hand has spent the same number of lifetimes really ticked off! She has carried so much anger about what happened that she refused to acknowledge her path. I was able to clear my grief and she was able to release her anger – and we both found the sister we never knew we had, but always longed for.

Vilma's Story

Vilma came to me recently for help with a distressing physical problem. She had been belching uncontrollably for the last year and a half. She'd seen medical doctors and a succession of alternative healers to no avail. Another healer referred her to me. She came in and laid down on my table and really wasn't able to give me much information because the belching was so continuous. In fact, the more I worked on her the worse it got. I was seriously considering telling her that I couldn't help her either.

The only reason I kept working on her was, that in the back of my mind I remembered another healer telling me the story of his gift. He was a medical intuitive who got confirmation on the location and diagnosis of illness by belching. He said that in a past life he'd been a Chinese healer, in a sect with the anglicized name of The Belchers. I couldn't get his story out of my mind as I followed her Inner's lead and worked through her session. She, too, had been one of the Belchers in a lifetime in China, but some trauma had occurred that caused her to lose faith in herself and her abilities. In fact, the exact source of her force was "feeling powerless against the will of others."   Once I'd identified the cause, we began a series of treatments, including acupuncture. Nothing worked and the belching became more and more violent. I was becoming concerned for her at this point, when her Inner said that what she needed to do was to mentally create a bottle, to invite the past life being into it, cork it and give it to God. As soon as she did this, the belching stopped! I was blown away!

I was so amazed that I wouldn't let her leave, and I kept her talking for over twenty more minutes to make sure that the burps didn't return. During this time I asked her what exactly was happening in her life when the belching started. She said that she had decided to get a divorce from her husband and had taken her four children away for a vacation to Cancun. Upon their return, her oldest daughter informed her that she wanted to live with her father rather than with her. Vilma felt powerless under the will of the daughter and this had triggered the past life's return for healing.

I didn't hear from her for about a week. One morning she called, quite upset that she had done something "terrible" and the belching had returned. I asked her what she was doing when it happened and she told me that she had been looking at the photos from the Cancun trip. She came for another session– a past life in the Yucatan area where she was sacrificed in one of the sacred cenotes. It seems that she was promised great things– immortality and royalty for making the supreme sacrifice. In fact, what happened was that she died. She felt betrayed– part of her soul was left at that cenote. She had to find it and re–integrate it within herself. As that force was cleared, the belching left once more.

Vilma was being strongly led to return to Cancun for her birthday this year– to be in the pyramid at Chichen Itza once more. As we concluded the previous session, I received a message for her that she would receive the "keys" at that time. I was also given a meditation for her to do while she was in the pyramid. It was a heart meditation, and it came with the message that she was to stay centered in her heart for her entire trip. She was to see only peace and love and all would be well for her. Her whole story resonated with the information I had recently read in *The Keys Of Enoch*, concerning spiritual happenings that are about to take place involving the sacred pyramids in the Yucatan area. I immediately assumed that those were the keys in the message I received.

When she arrived at the pyramid, there were all sorts of problems. A torrential downpour had caused leaking and the electricity was off. The pyramid was closed for repairs. She was persistent, insisting that it was imperative that she be allowed in. Perhaps an activation did take place for her that day, but on a more literal level, when she was finally able to enter the pyramid, following much confusion and disappointment, she was allowed to go in alone and was given the keys to unlock an area that is off limits to tourists – the Temple Of The Jaguar.

She was able to go inside and actually touch the Jaguar. She also did the heart meditation work that I had given her while she was there. It was very powerful for her! When she returned to the United States, every time she closed her eyes for weeks, she was transported back to that temple. She had been given a hands–on healing modality that has enabled her to assist others in mending broken bones, easing migraines and relieving pain. It appears that she has awakened the learning and abilities that she had in those lifetimes, shamanic healing gifts from Mayan times!

Steven's Story

Steven came to me for sessions because he received a gift certificate for five sessions from his employees as a Christmas present. This group came up with this idea because one of them had been seeing me for a while and was aware of Steven's fascination with past lives. He really didn't think he had any "issues" he wanted to work on, he just wanted to know more about his incarnations and whether he'd had lifetimes with his parents and his brothers before. He said, "My oldest brother and I have had a really strained relationship in this life. We just have never gotten along. My mom and I were always really close, and I think part of the reason for the stress between us, is that he wasn't ever very nice to her– and I resented that."

In his first session, we began a string of past life clearings where he was abused by one or the other of his parents. In this incarnation, these forces have caused him to turn away from his inner guidance at a young age, as well as to have an aversion to change and not be able to express what's inside. His heart chakra was closed from this repeated mistreatment. The abusers in those lifetimes have been with him in this one as his mother, another his father and older brother. Needless to say, this probably explains why the relationships with his brother and father have been strained, and even though his mother abused him in a past life, he was quite close to her until she died two years ago.

It was interesting for me to watch the changes in this man over the weeks. He came every Thursday evening for months. In the beginning he was introverted, quiet and somewhat skeptical. In fact, I was surprised when at the end of his gift certificate he told me that he wanted to keep on working. It was almost as if that commitment made a difference to his Inner, because from that time forth, his sessions became more and more profound.

One night, we were dealing with an ancestral force– men on both sides of his family, way back in time. His therapy was to find both the ancestors and clean them up, restoring them to health. When I came back in the room after he had completed what he was supposed to do he looked at me in the strangest way. He said,

"Those men were right here! I felt them standing on either side on me. They put their hands over my eyes, though, because they said I wasn't supposed to actually see them." I told Steven, "You have been holding back on me– you can see dead people can't you?"

Sure enough, he admitted that he had been able to see spirits when he was a child, but it scared him and he'd stopped. In fact, he also shared that as a young child, he would pass perfect strangers on the street and instantly know everything about their lives. "It was too much information for me," he said, "I shut it down because it bothered me."

Steven missed his mother dearly. Almost every week, he'd ask me if I felt her presence. Many times, she was there, nodding or smiling as he let go of some of his emotional baggage. After the incident with the ancestors, I suggested that he begin to use his gifts once more. I asked him to invite his mother to be with him. It was such a touching reunion. She didn't say anything, but he saw her and felt her loving presence. I told him that he could pull her close any time he desired, but I think that still frightens him too much to do it.

Victoria's Story

I've probably done more sessions on Victoria than I have on anybody beside myself. She seemed to get so much from my sessions, that in the beginning she would come several times a week. Her first session was profound enough that she realized immediately the benefit she might receive from more work. She said, "You know, Jean, I've tried it all– breath work, hypnosis, therapy and more, but this work has moved more junk faster than anything else!" When she first came to me she wanted to work on relationship issues. She was in the process of getting her second divorce. She was fairly sure that this was in the best interest of both parties, but it had been dragging on for a while and she was anxious to get on with her life. Her first session was about feeling defenseless and unsafe and we began charting a course of ancestral and past life healing that would bring up for her many very deep and painful issues so that she could release them.

She had been a victim of child abuse at a very young age, and had created negative patterns around sex and money over the years to mask that pain. As she now says, "I had no clue who I really was, so how could I be in a relationship and present myself to anyone else. The biggest gift I've received from the InnerSpeak process is finding my real self".

After about a year of at least weekly sessions, Victoria decided that she needed to learn how to do the work herself. She's taken InnerSpeak to a new level! Her passion is feng shui, and she's created a set of InnerSpeak files that relate to the house and the feng shui bagua, helping her to assist clients in clearing the stuck energy in their homes and clearing the forces that surround their lives at the same time.

An added blessing is that about six months into her sessions, she and her husband decided to reconcile! She began to see that their separation was one of her own creations. They were together to help each other and their daughter heal, and the separation was allowing her to run away from that responsibility. While Gary has had to deal with his own issues of accepting Victoria as her authentic self, the good with the not so good, he's been generous and a source of unconditional love for her for the most part. He's now in the process of learning how to facilitate InnerSpeak sessions, as well, and Victoria continues to work on herself on a regular basis, clearing out the day–to–day issues that previously would have stonewalled her.

Now that you have a picture of how the process of discovery has been working successfully in the lives of many people through these vignettes, it is time to share a longer story. It is the path of one soul's lifting of pain. It happens to be my soul, but you will see yourself in the picture, I trust, for we are all on the same path. It is my hope that through the experiencing of this story, you will see how the process can work in the lives of those open to it, and that you will find hope and courage and gather insights to help you lift off your own pain and move forward. The journey doesn't have to be as long or as fraught with struggle as mine has been. As the consciousness of this planet rises, we are all moving through our issues faster and faster. The rewards of quickening, our awakenings, are worth the effort!

Part II
This Lifetime–Jean's Story

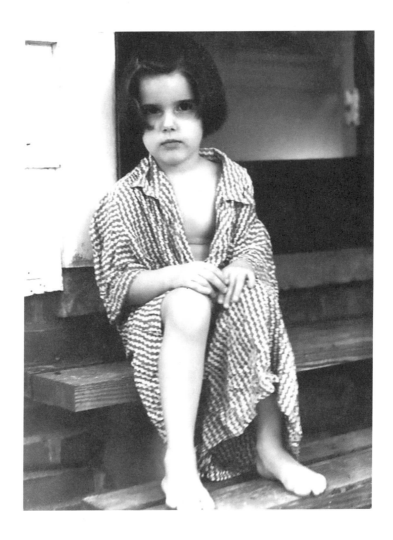

Chapter Four
The Resurrection

Once upon a time there was a little girl, and all she ever wanted was to be loved. Her heart was pure, and she loved all those around her, but she didn't really know what it would look like for her to receive it back. Over time she was able to get little glimpses, but pieces of the picture were always missing, and the experience of love always seemed to be just outside of her grasp. The year is now 2001 and this little girl is a fifty–three year old woman, a successful sales representative for a high–tech company. Her sales are up, she's on goal for the year and is taking a "break" lying on a table at a trendy salon having her legs waxed. For twenty–two years she's worked successfully in the telecommunications industry, earning well into six figures each year. She thrives in the competitive environment, because she's highly motivated and feels like she's providing solutions that her customers need rather than just selling them products. She's "good" at what she does, but it is becoming less and less satisfying to her.

The stress is beginning to take its toll physically, because she constantly worries that she might not be able to "make quota" or "keep her job." She also worries that her age is becoming an issue, because as the stress–related health problems like aching knees and arthritis in her hands have increased and her stamina has decreased, she frets that she just can't compete effectively with the younger, hungrier kids coming into the industry. Her world, as she knew it, came crashing down around her on April 30, 2001, that day in the salon, when her cell phone rang. It was her boss. He said, "Jean, I hate to do this, but I must tell you that we are paying everyone through close of business today and filing for bankruptcy reorganization of the company." Wow, just like that! How do you tell the esthetician to stop mid–wax because you have just lost your job and need to conserve every penny from this moment on? She probably should not have been surprised. Remember the old adage, "be careful what you ask for because you just might get it".

The Crisis

Several years earlier, she had begun to study with a local energy healer, to learn how to facilitate his healing work. She had been fascinated by his work since her first session many years before. She was led to him in 1990, while participating in an "annual" spring cleanse to detoxify her body. This process always commenced with a Saturday lecture by the doctor who was directing the cleanse. During the lunch break, several women went to a natural foods café and were sitting around the lunch table discussing "the weirdest and wildest metaphysical thing I've ever done."

One of the women said that she worked with a guy who did "energy work" and that he had changed her life. Of course, those words, "change my life" caught Jean's ear and she wanted to know more. When she asked what this man specifically "did" to change her life; the lady just couldn't put it into words. For some reason, she must have resonated with what she heard enough to ask for the healer's phone number. She wrote it in the back of her checkbook register and went on with the class, the cleanse and the rest of her life.   Perhaps a year later, she began having problems at work. She was a Senior Sales Representative for a local computer manufacturer. This was a "mom and pop" company that was very loosely managed. Most decisions were made "by the seat of someone's pants." Generally the decision maker was significantly less experienced than she was, and if it was a technical decision, they were also generally less technical. As a "double" Pisces, with Pisces rising along with her Sun in Pisces, she's natively good–natured with a really LONG fuse. It takes a lot to make her fly off the handle. This being said, she had reached a place at her job where she was becoming argumentative, even belligerent and angry with the ineptness of her co–workers– totally out of proportion to whatever the situation was that happened to be provoking her at the time. She had started crying at work, having to leave the building and go home to collect herself on a regular basis, sometimes several times a week.

Anger and fear were building up inside of her. She was angry about not being heard. When she tried to give advice or show how something might be handled more professionally, she spoke up, but fear would then come rushing in from thoughts that she might lose her job because of her outspoken behavior.

Then came the crisis. It was to be a catalyst for her healing, but she did not know then. At the time, it drove her over the edge. One afternoon as she was driving back to town from another city where she had been meeting with customers all day, she got a call from one of her clients who needed to have an order shipped out immediately. He had been told by her inside assistant that it wouldn't happen because he had an accounts receivable balance of $10, so his account was on credit hold. She called the accounting department on her cell phone and asked why a $10 dispute would hold up an order that would generate $60,000 in gross profit. It just didn't make sense to her, and anyway, she knew that the $10 receivable was actually because the company had incorrectly billed the client for sales tax, even though he was a reseller that was tax–exempt.

The clerk was rude and made a remark that sparked her anger yet again. "If you and the rest of you lazy sales people would get off your butts and sell something, I wouldn't have to worry so much about collections," the clerk yelled. Jean screamed into the phone, "F——you!" and hung up on the clerk, then she fell apart. She was SO upset that she had to pull her car to the side of the road so that she could cry. That was so unlike her, because as a seasoned professional, she usually operated at a much higher level. Suddenly she remembered that phone number in the back of her check register. She called, got an appointment, and proceeded to change her life.

Her appointment took about an hour. It was probably the strangest experience she'd ever had! This older man with waist length gray hair pulled back in a ponytail laid her out on a table, put her hands in strange positions, did something weird with his hands over her belly, tapped her on the forehead a lot, gave her some alcohol–tasting drops under her tongue (she later learned that these were Bach Flower Remedies), and told her a bizarre story: It seems that her anger was being stimulated by a kindred soul whom she did not know. Neither had she ever been aware of this soul's presence. This young woman lived in South America and was contemplating suicide. Because Jean was experiencing some of the same forces that were causing this young woman to want to kill herself, she was resonating with the young woman's pain. She was told to try to visualize her. Not being very creative, Jean thought, "Right, this will never happen!" But, when she shut her eyes, there was the young girl, all wrapped up in a cocoon–like shroud that was made up of her own religious beliefs, fixations, and old decisions. Jean was asked to unwrap her and set her free. As she did this, her own anger began to unwrap from around her. When she left the healer's office, the anger was gone. She felt surprisingly free, almost like she was her "real" self again. The angry identity that had been causing so many problems of late was gone, and she's had no problems with anger management since that day. She had no idea what this man had done to promote this shift. She had never heard of clinical kinesiology, and did not realize that was what he used with her.

As she processed what had occurred over the next few days, many questions came up. It was almost scary to think that we could be so influenced by something or someone that far removed from our conventional reality. However, she realized that she had found a healing modality that worked for her. Something clicked, and she "knew" at a deep inner level that she was supposed to be doing this type of work also.

This knowledge was frightening at first, because for so many years she had been comfortably operating from her left–brain in the black and white corporate world that she'd become so used to. She had lost contact with her intuitive abilities and her spiritual path, for that matter, and it certainly seemed like this work involved healing on a psychic, if not spiritual level. She had been through several years of traditional psychotherapy to heal childhood issues and had always dealt with health crises via traditional allopathic medicine. In fact, she even looked upon chiropractic as fairly far out in left field, although she did credit it with working. She had no experience or training in the realms of healing therapy, but she had always been fascinated with medicine and related things. Even though she had an undergraduate degree in psychology, she certainly did not feel qualified in any way to take on such a task!

As time went on and issues came up for her, she'd return to this energy healer and he would work on her. She would shift and change. Sometimes the shifts were profound, more often than not, they were quite subtle. After a while she asked him, "Are you a psychic?" and "What exactly enables you to accomplish such healing?" He sort of blew the question off by telling her, "I was a stockbroker and a corporate type before I found this body of work through a healing crisis of my own." Something inside told her that she wanted – needed – to learn how to do it, too. She asked him to train her, and he agreed.

At the time she lost her job in 2001, she had been studying with this man for several years and was about to finish up ten months of practitioner training, which would certify her to begin healing work on her own if she so chose. This was what she really wanted to do, and she had been agonizing over how it might be possible to make such an enormous career transition.

She was happily married to a man with a great job, but they had always agreed that they would be a "two–career" family, and he did not see this "healing adventure" of hers as a valid career! Her husband called her healing work a "hobby that she should pursue in addition to a real job." How could she walk away from the income potential and life style she was used to and face starting a business from scratch – on faith alone? This was an element of sacrifice that she grappled with daily, if not hourly for months, and always in the background was her husband's chant, "Keep your day job, keep your day job!"

The Universe gifted her with the opportunity she had dreamed of and asked for, the perfect place to begin a new career. Her job had just ended and the economy was in such a downturn that there wasn't a replacement job in her industry. She had nothing to lose and so very much to gain! At this point she had begun the job of clearing not only the traumas from her lifetime, but also removing forces she carried forward from past lives and forces that were inherited from her ancestors as well. She was well on the way of releasing the past patterns of victimhood and opening the channels to a much more creative and joyful life. The journey had been an arduous one, however. Jean found herself pondering. She was amazed she had come so far in such a relatively short period of time. Even more amazing was the realization that this lifetime is an infinitesimally small portion of the journey. It was time to go back. It was time to put all the puzzle pieces together.

Chapter Five
The Separation

The Early Years: Disappearing

Most of us are born into this lifetime with hearts open and expecting to be loved. We are clean slates, ready to experience life and learn. Then, it seems, fate conspires to separate us from that original state of grace, and we spend our whole lifetime striving to reclaim it and find our way back home. Jean was no exception. Jean Adrienne Miller was born 54 years ago to a couple that was fairly advanced in age to be starting a family. Her mother was forty at her birth. Her mother told her father when they married that she was too old to have children. He was ok with that because he said he really didn't want kids anyway.

Her mother's family hailed from Arkansas. Mildred, her mother, was the oldest of four girls, raised by Jean's grandmother as a single parent. Mildred's father died from typhoid fever when she was seven years old. Mildred was independent, as might be expected from her upbringing. She was one of the original "women's libbers," moving to Florida in the 1940's to work for the Department of Agriculture in the new field of seed testing. She helped develop Florida's standards for purity and germination in seed samples required by farmers before they are able to sell their seeds. She actually opened the first commercial seed–testing laboratory in Florida in 1950. She completed her college degree in botany while she was pregnant with Jean.

Jean's father's family was from a farming area south of Tallahassee. John, her father, was one of six children, and both of his parents were dead before she was born. John was quite a bit younger than Mildred and was extremely handsome. He never finished high school because he had to work to help support his family. He served in the US Navy Seabee organization in the South Pacific during World War II and returned to Florida to take care of his aging mother and to earn a living selling electrical supplies. Suffice it to say, their relationship was fiery! The little girl that came into the world wanting just to be loved grew up in an atmosphere of yelling, glass throwing, accusation slinging, and overheard inappropriate slandering. Mildred spent a lot of time frustrated with John. They were so different. She was a driven woman from a young age.

In fact, she probably was an undiagnosed example of bi–polar disorder. She wanted things done on her timeframe, and John was not overly motivated. They both had hot tempers. He was methodical and neat; she operated from her instincts and didn't always pay attention to the details. Her self–esteem was low and she lived in fear and jealousy. He was extremely good–looking, and whether real or imagined, she always thought he was flirting with other women. She was an educated botanist with an ample supply of petri dishes for germinating seeds. When she reached the boiling point because of something he'd done or something she imagined he'd done, she'd explode into a tantrum and smash them by the hundreds. As Jean grew older, it became her chore to clean up the mess. She became a sounding board for Mildred's fears, as she was brought into discussions about Mildred's desire to leave or her concerns that John was "running around" on her. What Jean was never able to clean up, though, were the emotional scars from those outbursts and the inappropriate conversations of a dysfunctional family. This little girl that only wanted to be loved became very frightened. The accusations and threats took away all sense of security as she got older. Her only salvation is that most of this either didn't exist when she was quite small, or she was just too young to realize what was happening then. Jean's first five years were delightful. She was an only child then, with her Grandmother Henry (Granny) living with the family, her Aunt Lil (Mildred's sister) living nearby, and her beloved maid, Flossie May Conyers, doting on her constantly. She was the first grandchild and the only baby living in the area on either side of her family. Flossie dressed her smartly, braided her lovely hair, and put pretty bows in it every day. The few "problems" in the early years revolved around either Mildred's traveling on business or the friction between John and Granny. The good thing about Granny living with them was that she was there to take care of Jean in the evenings while Mildred worked or traveled and after Flossie left for the day. The bad side was that she was sloppy, and this drove John to distraction!

Also, when Jean was five, her brother, Jake, was born and the dynamics changed in their house. The attention that she had received from her dad quickly shifted to her brother, and she began a downward spiral into the trap of "I'm not good enough." This was reinforced in many ways.

Instead of greeting his daughter with a hug and a kiss, he'd yell, "Jean, how many times do I have to tell you to put your shoes away!" She felt as though she couldn't do anything "right." She didn't remember displays of affection, but she did remember having to go into the yard to pick the switch that would be used for punishment, or having to go to his closet to get the belt that would be used to beat her.

When Jean heard her daddy coming home, instead of feeling glad, she cringed. "Here we go again," the eight–year–old girl thought. She hid in her bedroom, where she usually hid during a tempest. John stormed into the house from the seed laboratory. He'd looked through the mail and found where Mildred had been on a shopping spree once again. He was ranting about the lack of money and her complete disregard for it, and Mildred yelled back, "Well, damn it, I make it and I can damn well spend it if I want to!" They would carry on until Mildred got tired or until she'd started throwing things. Then, John would take out his frustration on the kids. He'd tear into Jean's room and yell about its disarray. Sometimes he'd hit her; sometimes she would escape with the criticism.

All her desires about love were dashed with each critique, and she began to believe that nothing she did would ever make her "good enough" to please him. She couldn't remember how old she was when she just quit caring. She never quit trying to please, but she became disconnected from the results. Later in life as a woman, one day she had a major realization. One of her clients was a critical old lady who berated her for not wearing enough makeup to not dressing in the style she deemed appropriate. She kept returning and suffering along with the abuse for several months until it hit her– she was still trying to please her long–deceased and difficult father!

She knew what she must do. Her stomach churned at the thought of what she must say, she began sweating, but she picked up the phone anyway. "Lou, this is Jean. I really don't think that there is anything further that I can do for you. All of your solutions are within yourself, and you must look there and do what is necessary. It is a waste of your money and my time to continue your sessions." It was like the weight of the world had been lifted from her shoulders. As she sighed with relief, she knew that she was finally breaking the legacy of abuse.

There was a plus to having a younger brother. Until Jake was old enough – out of diapers and able to fend for himself, Jean was Daddy's girl. She was taught how to shoot a shotgun she could barely hold up, and she "got" to go hunting with the men. It was SO boring to be taken out into a field and left for hours alone with just that shotgun.

She tried all manner of things to fill the time and avoid becoming scared...building cities in the sand and wandering around aimlessly. She was cold and hungry. There was no place to go to the bathroom. Finally, she just sat in the sand and cried until she fell asleep. When John finally came to get her, just before dark, he yelled at her for getting sand in the gun and not staying where he had left her. Jake became his daddy's hunting companion, and she was freed from that awful responsibility!

Mildred was generally focused on her work, so attention and demonstrations of affection were scarce from her as well. One day when she was in the third grade, at school, Jean had won first place at the school–wide spelling bee. She ran into the seed laboratory, excited. Her mother was bent over her desk in the middle of a purity examination on a sample of seeds. "Mom?" she said, hating to interrupt. "Guess what, Mom?" At this, Mildred looked up and said, "Don't you know I'm in the middle of the busy season? Don't bother me now! Go fix your brother some supper." She shrugged her shoulders and turned away so that her mother wouldn't see the tears that she was fighting back. "One day you'll notice me," she thought.

She was too little to realize that her mother had been the primary breadwinner throughout her life and lived in fear of not having enough money to put food on the table or pay the bills. Much of the love and attention the little girl did receive had conditions attached – ""If you do this for me, I'll…" or "how could you do that if you really loved me." It's hard for a child to separate the truth from appearances, so little Jeannie began to believe that she was not important and that all love has strings attached to it.

School Years: Striving Painfully

So, she rapidly became an over–achiever, striving to gain attention and approval by being the smartest, most talented, cutest, whatever… always made straight A's, played the piano and almost every instrument in the band, danced, sang, cleaned, cooked and worked in the seed laboratory. The place where she seemed to get the most recognition was in school, and in order to garner that much desired praise, sometimes she cut corners. For example, she would skim through books so that she could win the award for reading the most books during the semester.

In the third grade, Jean's teacher decided that she should be moved mid–year to the fourth grade because she was scholastically ahead of her class. At first she was excited by this prospect. It represented success and individual attention. What she didn't realize was the cost she would pay for this. Once again, she was an outsider. In her new fourth grade class, she became the smarty–pants nerd stuck in a room with thirty older kids she didn't know.

They were cold and unmerciful. She went from being the most popular girl in her class to the least. In her old class, the cutest boy in the room, Jeff, had a crush on her. It was the last crush she experienced until high school. Perhaps it shouldn't be a surprise that shortly after she was moved up, her vision began to fail. Within two months she couldn't read the blackboard. She didn't understand what was happening to her. Her feelings of disorientation that were associated with the promotion were beginning to aspect her completely. Every day she would come home from school tired, sad and with a terrible headache. Eventually, her mother figured out what was going on and had her eyes examined. Now she was the nerd with glasses!

While this strategy of getting attention by succeeding in school enabled her to get through college by age 18, it did very little for her self–esteem! She'd managed to grow academically and even culturally very well, but emotionally she was extremely immature. While she had friends over the years, she never had an exclusive best friend, but was always the third member of a trio and got left out a lot. There were no children her age in her neighborhood to play with after school and on the weekends, so school was truly her only outlet for "play." This forced separation from her friends placed her, once again, into a hostile environment and removed her outlet that allowed her to be a child. She carried this phenomenon forward until she reached middle age.

Church: Outcast from Love

About the only thing in Jean's life that was a constant was Church. What could have meant love, or what should have been a good thing, turned into a nightmare. In the beginning, John and Mildred didn't go to church regularly, so Granny insisted on taking her to church every Sunday. This was interesting, because John's mother had also been one of the founders of the Methodist Church in Woodville, the little town just south of Tallahassee where he was raised.

Florrie, his mother, was full of "fire and brimstone," so it was said, and probably if she'd been living at the time, they wouldn't have missed a Sunday at her church, and there would have been a battle with Granny over who would get the grandchild on Sunday morning! From as early as Jean could remember, however, her daddy DID require them to attend Easter Sunrise services. How she hated getting up so early, in the cold and dark, for something she totally didn't understand! Only the promise of the candy from the Easter Bunny waiting at home made it bearable!

After Jake was born, their daddy "got religion" and joined the Methodist Church in Tallahassee. The family became a fairly fundamental Christian family. Thus began the era of having to go to Sunday school every Sunday, and to church on all Sundays except the first one of the month (when they served communion – John hated that part for some reason.) The rule was, you went unless you were really sick – you know, doctor's excuse sick!

Jean's little heart beat faster with anticipation. God is about love. Churches are full of Christian people. Maybe here is the place where she can find the love her little heart is aching for! Her high hopes began sinking as they drove further and further away from their neighborhood. The church her parents had chosen was on the opposite side of town. As they walked into the church, she looked frantically around for one familiar face. There was none. All the kids in Jean's Sunday school class were from different schools than the one she attended. She gathered up her courage to enter the Sunday school room she had been assigned to. As usual, everybody looked at the "new girl" and snickered. One of the other girls even made a remark about her dress. She began to learn a different lesson there, about being an outcast, not fitting in. The words to the song "Jesus Loves Me" mocked her. She began to dread Sunday mornings.

She kept looking to find the expression of God's love at church, but her search was daunted. When she murmured, "Our Father, Who art in heaven..." in the Lord's Prayer, pictures of her earthly father kept popping into her head. On a good day, he was not very approving of her, and at church, it just became worse. A lot of what goes on at church goes over the head of a kid, and boredom slipped in quite easily. On the coattails of boredom followed chastisement for misbehaving. Jean was the lucky one in her family, though, because she was so afraid of her daddy's disapproval, she really worked at being "invisible." Jake, on the other hand was younger, wilder and just a "boy." He had a really hard time.

Every Sunday when they got home from church, without fail, John pulled him into the bathroom and gave him a beating with the belt for "cutting up" in church. He never seemed to be bothered by it. He'd just march right in and take his punishment. It's amazing that Jake still goes to church! In fact, it's even more amazing that he didn't turn out even more screwed up than Jean did. The point here is that somewhere along the way, Jean got really confused about

God's love – and got really angry with Him for the lack of love she felt in her life.

Food As The Unfulfilling Comfort

At an early age food became her comfort and reward. Every afternoon after school, Mildred would take the kids to the local "five and dime" for a coke and egg custard pie. At other times when boredom set in, they'd go to the bakery and the three of them would consume an entire lemon chess pie, or napoleons or whatever was on sale. On Sundays, the family usually went to Morrison's Cafeteria, downtown, for dinner (between church and the weekly beating session – in the South, the three meals are breakfast, dinner and supper.)   The kids were allowed to order whatever they wanted, including dessert. This indulgence helped her to put off thinking about the "inevitable." Her knowledge that Jake was about to get beaten engendered her with the fear that she might as well. By the sixth grade she was severely overweight.

The darker side of her relationship with food revolved around the kitchen table. There was generally some type of conflict going on during meals – "don't sing at the table" or even outright fighting between the two kids, or between John and Jake. Mealtimes became a battlefield that included making the kids sit at the table until they had cleaned their plates. It was a source of struggle two and sometimes three times a day.

She learned to cope with loneliness and disappointment by eating – everything she could put her hands on when she was at home. There the loneliness took its toll. At least at school, there were kids her own age to be around, and some of the time there was positive socialization, but after school, there was just work, homework, TV, eating, and trying to stay out of the ever present "trouble." By the time she reached twenty, she had MAJOR issues: addictive personality, relationship problems, social alienation, and a rocky relationship with her family members.

Boys?

She'd never had a boyfriend (not hard to figure since she had a weight problem until the ninth grade!) She spent too many idle hours dreaming about this boy or that boy, imagining how it might feel to have that first kiss. As she got fatter, she became the brunt of some cruel jokes. One evening, the phone rang, and it was for HER. She never got calls. Tentatively, she said, "Hello?" On the other end of the line was a voice that purported to be Dickie, one of the cutest boys in her sixth grade class. She had a really big crush on him. "So, Jean," the raspy voice said. "I want to know if you would like to go steady with me." "Wwwwell, I guess so," she stammered. The voice replied, "OK, tomorrow when we get to school, I'll give you my ID bracelet to wear." Jean was elated – finally, she would have a boyfriend and get to wear one of the coveted ID bracelets! She was thrilled beyond belief until she got to school the next day and found everybody snickering at her. One of the girls in her class, one that she thought was her friend, had called her up and with a disguised voice was pretending to be Dickie. It was a cruel joke, and almost everyone in her class – both the girls and the boys were in on it. Her heart was broken. She stayed home sick and cried for days.

When she was a sophomore in high school love entered her life. His name was Rocky. This first boyfriend, Rocky, was a dear. He worshipped her and she ate it up! This was one of those peeks at being loved, a glimpse that lasted almost three years. Together, through trial and error, they learned about life, relationships and sex. They went to the beach, the prom, and spent months at the drive–in movies. Rocky's parents accepted her into their family like one of their own children. His mom taught her how to cook great Italian meals and she watched his dad create gastronomic delights on the grill. She saw that meals could be a loving experience, filled with fun. She spent most of her spare time with Rocky and his family and she began to lose weight. Within a year, she was tiny, had a gorgeous figure and got a lot of attention she had never received before.

Jean finished high school in three years, because Rocky was two years ahead of her in school and they wanted to get married. The truth is, she saw marriage as a way to escape her dysfunctional family life, a way to "belong" to a "normal," happy, loving family. Mildred, in a brilliant move altogether, refused to allow this until she had a college degree. This just caused Jean to set her jaw more firmly.

She talked to the principal at the high school and the Dean of Students at FSU. Neither one could come up with any reason why she couldn't leave high school and start college early, so Jean completed her high school education in three years and enrolled in college. Anything to move her closer to her escape! Consequently, at sixteen, she was significantly younger than her peers in age (and light years younger in social and emotional skills.) The relationship with Rocky didn't even make it through her freshman year – there were so many boys at FSU to choose from! Hindsight says that it wasn't meant to last anyway, but it was there to help her grow and see that love was possible for her to experience. It's just unfortunate that it took another thirty years for her to find that unconditional love and acceptance again from anyone besides her children and pets. In college, she found cigarettes and alcohol and used them instead as tools to help her "fit in".

She had no clue what she wanted to do with her life, she was only sixteen, and relatively few kids at that age do. Mildred, however, was sure that teaching was a respectable career choice for her. She had excelled in Spanish in high school, which enabled her to exempt half the Spanish courses required for a bachelors degree, so Spanish with an education minor was how she was registered. She didn't understand the Greek program, but Mildred thought she should be in a sorority. Mildred began an analysis of the sororities at FSU, researching each one thoroughly, based on historical data, not based on the personalities in the chapters at FSU. She thought that since Alpha Phi was the oldest, it must be the "best" one, so that's where Jean pledged, and because everything always works out the way it's supposed to, she learned very powerful lessons there, not just through the group of girls she met, but also through the process that got her there. Basically, she gave up her power at age sixteen, by allowing her mother to choose her education and associations, and wasn't able to reclaim it again until she was fifty–two.

While she had "fun" during college, with lots of dates, dancing and beer drinking, it was a lonely time for her. As the youngest in the sorority, she was once again the brunt of jokes and was taken advantage of quite often because of her naiveté. Relationships with the opposite sex didn't go much better. The high school boyfriend lasted until the spring of her freshman year, when she threw him over in order to attend a fraternity party with a blind date so that she could get a blanket with the fraternity crest on it. Sad...

One of the "rules" Mildred had for her at FSU was that she was supposed to call home everyday. Being a typical teenager, she was busy and forgetful, as seventeen–year–olds usually are, so it became her pattern that by Friday she'd forget to make that call. When she'd get in from her Friday night date there would be a note on her mirror saying, "Pack your bags, your dad will pick you up at 6AM – they are taking you out of the sorority and out of school." She'd work at home all day Saturday, doing chores and helping in Mildred's seed laboratory and they'd kiss and make up by 4PM. She would be back at the sorority house in time to go out on Saturday night. This went on, like clockwork, for an entire year! Jean was so desperate to fit in. One of the goals she set for herself was to have a date every Friday and Saturday night. She didn't care who the guy was; she just didn't want to sit home. It was bad enough staying in at the sorority house, with the "geeks that could-n't get dates," even worse when she was living at home and need-ed to escape. Remembering that nice girls "don't," Jean made sure the worse thing that happened on these dates was generally beer drinking and necking. By her junior year, she was drinking almost every night. Luckily, she was going dancing almost every night, as well, and the dancing, together with running between classes on FSU's large campus, helped her to maintain a slim profile. The dates and the few "relationships" they produced were superficial. Most of the guys, she really didn't like. There were a few that were special, like Andy, but they were special for all the wrong reasons.

There was a girl in her sorority that she really didn't get along with, Ida May. It was just one of those personality conflicts, no real reason for it. Ida May was a few years ahead of Jean. She had dated Andy, who had just graduated and gotten drafted. She talked about him a lot, making him out to be some great hero. Andy was a Sigma Nu. Their frat house was right next door to Alpha Phi, Jean's sorority. It was the Sigma Nu weekend that sealed the breakup of Jean and Rocky, and she went on a blind date to it with a boy named Kenny, a really nice guy. Unfortunately for Kenny (and Ida May, as well), he broke his leg playing intramural football the day before the big weekend. "How could he?" thought Jean selfishly, "This means I'll have to sit on the sidelines and won't get to dance. Bummer!"

And so it was, but halfway through the Friday night dance, which was held on the Sigma Nu's basketball court behind their house, in full view of the bedroom windows on one side of the Alpha Phi house, who should saunter in but Andy.

Their eyes met before he reached the center of the room – chemistry! He asked her to dance, and Kenny reluctantly said ok. Before the evening was over, Kenny was history and Jean was Andy's date for the rest of the Weekend's festivities. Jean was in "luv," but certainly not in love.

Monday morning, it was back to classes. She pulled first one dress and then another from her closet. The hems were torn out of each one. How could that be? They were fine on Friday. Ida May was a home economics major, and this was her best jab at revenge. She had been sure that Andy would take HER to the weekend when he got back to Tallahassee on leave from the Army.

Jean showed her! Within a week, she was wearing Andy's fraternity pin. Within another week, she had given it back. It seems that the Sigma Nu's had a saying, "When you are lavaliered, your near. When you are pinned, you're in!" Well, being the "nice girl" meant that she would have no part of that. Regardless, she and Ida May gave each other wide berth for the next year.

She graduated from the Florida State University at eighteen with a degree in a field she had no interest in and the maturity of a fifteen year old. She entered the workforce, once again significantly younger than her peers. Mildred told her she was too young to move away to work (probably true,) so she was led by her mom to the State of Florida Merit System to take all the merit exams she was qualified for. Jean aced all the tests she took and ended up with a choice of several jobs, and accepting the one that paid the most – economic statistician. She sold out for the highest dollar. Once she had a job and her own source of income, the next thing on her agenda was to get out of the family house – FREEDOM! She found an opening where three girls she didn't know needed a roommate and she moved into her first apartment. This upset Mildred terribly. It's clear now that she came into this life to work on issues with both parents, but in particular, several InnerSpeak sessions exposed an interesting twist. Each of us chooses our parents prior to incarnating to facilitate learning the lessons we need to grow spiritually. It seems that Jean made a conscious choice for a mother while in spirit, that her earthly mother would be her Aunt Lil. Before her descent into incarnation, though her soul realized that she might not have the opportunity to learn the lessons that were part of her contract, so Plan B was instituted.

How this took place, no one knows, but three souls agreed to this change. Jean incarnated into the family of John and Mildred. Probably, Mildred had no idea what she'd signed up for! Jean scared the daylights out of her.

There was some aspect of Jean's light and power that she didn't understand, and at some level she was jealous of it. She shut it down through control. For the first eighteen years of her life. Mildred never loosened her grip. She reluctantly let Jean spend so much time at Aunt Lil's, probably because she had other agendas anyway, and many times would exhibit jealousy if Jean were gone too long. Moving out brought up all Mildred's forces around that choice and the potential of losing control. In another fit of temper, she itemized all the money that had been spent on Jean's education and presented her with a bill. Jean was still giving her a check for $50 a month to repay this "debt" when Mildred died eleven years later. Talk about giving away one's power! They created this "game" and it became so comfortable that they continued it for years, truthfully until Mildred's death.

It wouldn't be fair to only share the negative aspects of John and Mildred. Jean's life was not all misery. There were good times along the way. Positive traits were inherited and learned from both parents. John had a naturally good singing voice. Mildred had studied piano and the humanities and she imparted music appreciation to go along with singing ability for Jean. She studied piano from the time her little hands were big enough to reach an octave on the keyboard and took dancing lessons from kindergarten on. Before she left high school, she had mastered almost all of the instruments in the band. John got the family to church, but Mildred taught spirituality. She had Jean read *As A Man Thinketh* when she was ten. She didn't understand what she had read for another forty years! Mildred was a role model for independence and character for her.

Her parents sacrificed so that she could receive the

well–rounded platform that would support her in the years to come. They cut corners to enable her to go to FSU's summer band and majorette camps from junior high through high school. They allowed her to join a sorority, which was a luxury that would tax even a wealthier family's budget. She had all the material comforts anyone could want. She just couldn't find the satisfaction of the unconditional love she so yearned for.

Chapter Six
The Marriages

Her first marriage came at the respectable age of twenty–one (going on about sixteen) to a man eight years her senior. She married him because he was available. She wanted to have children, and she just KNEW she was going to end up an "old maid." Almost every one she knew was already married for crying out loud! Life outside the family home wasn't as easy as she'd thought, either. Supporting oneself, paying bills and buying food and clothes wasn't as fun as it had looked from the other side of the fence. Getting married also appeared to be the way out of that "rat–race."

John had good genes. He was great looking and had the build of a football player, which he had been in college. He was a bit more conservative than most of the guys she'd gone out with before – and a whole lot older. His mother had fixed them up. She worked in the same office with Jean. He was living in Washington State at the time and was coming home for a holiday. He went back after a couple of weeks, and a few dates. They corresponded, but nothing more happened until his brother–in–law was killed in the Viet Nam war. Their family was devastated. John left his job in Washington and returned to Tallahassee to take care of his sister. At that time they resumed dating. It was more perfunctory than anything else. There were no bells, little excitement. But it was comfortable, he was nice, and he had the potential to be a good provider.

Looking back, it's easy to see why that marriage couldn't last.

They were from different poles, and while they say that opposites attract, there has to be some commonality for a relationship based on opposites to last. They did produce two great kids. That is probably the ONLY reason the Universe brought them together! This man was critical, conservative and undemonstrative. He had "rules": save every penny, don't waste. "We can't afford" meant make all your clothes and all the kids clothes. It meant, "You are not allowed to go bowling with the other moms in the neighborhood." After she went back to work when their youngest was almost two, he demanded meals on the table and a clean house, but never offered to help. "My God," thought Jean. "I've married my father! They even have the same name!"

I am continually amazed, not just by my own experience but from those of my clients, how we can repeatedly do such things that are obviously not in the best interest of our souls. She cried every day for the first year they were married.

The sadness was profound, because the reality of the situation she had created was setting in day by day – out of the frying pan and into the fire. The little girl that wanted love so desperately had replicated the scenario she'd lived for about thirteen of her years on the planet.

After a year, she got pregnant. Things got better after a while when her son, Robby was born. What a gift a baby is! From those beautiful eyes came the looks of unconditional love she'd always craved. The connection that is achieved while the baby is at the breast cannot be equaled. She stayed home with him for over a year. When finances necessitated that she return to the workplace, she immediately became pregnant again – overnight! She wanted to re–capture the blissful feelings that the newborn had once given her. The glow was more short–lived the second time around. The stress of caring for two babies gets in the way, and it wasn't long before the tears and isolation were there once more.

By the time her youngest, Amanda, was out of diapers, she knew she couldn't stay in the marriage. Her needs were not being met. While she had grown up a lot in seven years, he was pretty much in the same place he was when they married. They tried counseling, but got nowhere. Her heart really wasn't in it. In the divorce, she wanted out so badly that she took on all their debt, thinking that he wouldn't hassle about custody of the children if she did. Wrong! Hassle her, he did. While he had never taken any interest in the day–to–day care of the kids, he decided that he wanted custody of them. This man that never changed a diaper or fed either one of them felt he was the better parent. This was com-plicated by the fact that he was a manager with the department of family and children's services and had contacts high up in the chain there. She was investigated at length. After significant harassment, which deepened her basic fears of separation and loss, she was judged to be a competent parent and retained primary cus-tody. But again the damage was done. She gave up her power again, by settling on taking the debt and minimal child support as trade for her freedom. And once again, that freedom she saw from the other side of the fence was not as exciting as it had appeared to be. She lost sixty pounds, moved to Atlanta and took a relatively well paying position with a major corporation, but it's even harder making ends meet as a single parent with a corporate job. It's hard-er to find companionship after you leave your area of familiarity. Life became a struggle of a different sort.

Her second attempt at marriage was with a British citizen who wanted a green card more than a long–term relationship. If her mother had not died a few months before she met this man, this relationship would never have gotten off the ground. Since she was still operating under Mildred's control until she passed, Jean went a "little nuts" so to speak. They met in a bar. He had shoulder–length curly hair and looked like a rock star.

His British accent made anything that came out of his mouth sound melodious, even the F–word (which punctuated most of his sentences.) Graham was a "child–man" and probably less mature than either of her children, but he re–introduced her to her Inner Child, one that had been filed away during all those years of learning how to take care of herself. They began to have fun, and together they discovered water sports and international travel. They went back to England every Christmas for several weeks, and she was able to explore that country. It was a shame she hadn't discovered InnerSpeak and all her past lives, because over half of them lived in England. Perhaps that was why she found this man so attractive.

She enjoyed being fearless and living on the edge. It felt GOOD! For the first time in her life, she was able to do as she pleased, and she didn't limit herself in any way. They bought a pool table and she learned to play. They bought Jet Skis, customized them, and she became daring, learning to do tricks on hers. They bought a boat and she learned to water ski – even wrote an article for WaterSki magazine on how to teach people to slalom, based on her own difficulties in learning. They bought scuba equipment and went through all the PADI certifications. This was more of a challenge since Graham hardly knew how to swim. Unfortunately, the gilt began to wear off and life started not being so much fun. She got tired of raising three kids. It became harder to keep her husband entertained than it did the "other" children. Graham really didn't want to work, and eventually decided he wanted to become a "professional" scuba diver. He took a job at a local dive shop. When he started spending more on dive gear than his paycheck, Jean decided to pull the plug, and opted out of the relationship. He got the toys and she kept her sanity (sort of) and added on a bunch more debt. As Aunt Lil said when they divorced, "Honey, I don't want to hear you complain. You got your money's worth from that one!"

There was a pattern developing here! She had no clue what love looked like, but she wanted it desperately. As the Universal Law of Correspondence works, the more she yearned for it the farther away she pushed it.

Marriage gave validity to sex and made it ok. In today's world, she would have probably just had affairs, but in the seventies that wasn't socially acceptable. Besides, she was raised with the belief that "nice girls don't."

Her third marriage was the shortest and most disastrous. She married a man several years her junior. Turned out he was a psychopath. It started out innocently enough – she was nearing forty, single parent and lonely when she got the bright idea to make a list of what she wanted in a husband and asked God to provide him. The problem was that she didn't understand the Universal Laws at this point – they just don't teach them in Episcopal Sunday School! (By the time she finished college she had decided to really push Daddy's buttons by changing denominations.) She made a "wish list" describing the man she thought she wanted. God's answer to us is always a resounding "Yes", and God gave her exactly what she asked for: handsome, well–educated, Episcopalian, spiritual, good job. She neglected to put sane on her list, so God neglected to provide her with a sane man. They dated for a year, but she didn't recognize who he truly was until they were leaving the church to the strains of the wedding march. She had seen that he was a little quirky. Both her kids said, "Mom, this guy's weird, he's nerdy and just not right." But she didn't listen. Her friends Nancy and Jill had both seen the real monster. Nancy told Jill, "We love her. We really need to put a stop to this before it goes too far and she gets hurt – or worse." Jill replied, "I know, but you know that she won't "hear" us really. What can we do?" And they kept their thoughts to themselves. She and Tom took a vacation to the Bahamas that summer, and things didn't go as smoothly as she would have liked. He became moody and somewhat unpleasant, but she dismissed what was going on and blamed herself for not doing whatever it was that he wanted, or for doing what it was that set him off. One night, the sex took a decidedly kinky turn. He began tying her hands to the bedposts with her underwear. She thought, "Geez, this can't really be happening to me!" But he wouldn't stop, no matter what she said, even though she was crying the whole time. That really should have gotten her thinking, but alas, again she figured she must be the prude he accused her of being. It had to be her fault, you know. They were married in December, began counseling in February and were divorced by August.

They had the "Honeymoon From Hell." They went skiing in Jackson Hole Wyoming, one of the most beautiful places in the world (and certainly not hell). It seemed as if he was on a quest to find out what she wanted to do, so he could insist that they do the opposite. He even refused to ski with her or meet her during the day, because he said she couldn't keep up with him on the slopes and he didn't want to be held back. Sex became more and more of an issue. Pretty soon, he didn't want to have sex unless he'd emotionally battered her until she was in tears. Here's the point. Every time the Universe gives you a lesson and you don't get it, the stakes are raised and the lesson gets more painful until it finally gets your attention! That marriage got her attention finally, but because she'd missed so many of the lessons as they were presented, it was pretty nasty at the end. After three months of counseling, the therapist told them to get a divorce, that he couldn't justify taking any more of their money! Finally she was put on the path to heal herself and figure out what she's really supposed to do in this lifetime.

There was a bright spot though – remember, everything does happen for a reason. This man had been heavily involved in the LRT (Loving Relationships Training) and introduced her to Rebirthing. She took the LRT weekend, and while she did not consciously understand the healing path she was embarking on, she got started healing on her inner pain. The first steps were taken, and experience now tells that once the seed of spiritual growth is planted and a commitment is made, God will grow that seed and assist us in walking the path.

In the divorce she also got custody of his copy of *A Course In Miracles* and began the 365–day workbook exercises. The Course was a major turning point in her life – she began to take responsibility for her life (the good and the bad) for the first time. For the first time, she was able to see that she was the one creating the reality that she was living. Seeing is not necessarily remembering on a daily basis, but she was beginning to wake up from the dream and that the Course made her aware that she had been living in. The Course piqued her interest in things spiritual.

After that divorce, she began a four–year course of study with The University of the South (Episcopal Seminary) called Education For Ministry. The other reason why she became an Episcopalian, besides making her dad angry, was because it was the first denomination she found that could state emphatically what they believed in a way that she could understand.

This little girl that only wanted to be loved had felt so spiritually lost for most of her life that this church became a good anchor. The Methodist church probably does the same thing, but it fell on deaf ears as she was growing up. There was just too much baggage in the way. With EFM, she was able to broaden her horizons. She was able to study not only what Episcopalians believe, but also learned what most of the other major religions held as truth. It comes back to the "Father" thing. Her issues with her earthly father made her want to make sure, really sure, that she was dealing with spirituality right – she didn't want to make that "angry Guy up there" disapprove of her any more. In fact, if there was a way to work up the ladder of "salvation" through ministry, she was going to give it a shot!

Life had started to look like a constant struggle by this time. In her thirty's her addictive behavior shifted from drinking and partying to excessive spending. She was so desperate for some measure of "respectability" that she bought fancy clothes, expensive jewelry, fast cars, even a boat or two to make the impression she so desired. Over the years between marriages two and three, she had amassed enormous debt trying to raise two kids by herself while trying to buy respectability. In fact, the debt became the secret that she kept hidden from everyone. Her third husband was married to her for almost a year and never had a clue! Some people hide alcoholism or drugs; Jean hid the shame of debt. It became the source of all her stress. The debt became the symbol of the self–sabotage she was doing. She even considered bankruptcy as a way out of the downward spiral, but just before she did that, she finally decided to take responsibility for the mess she'd made. She found the Consumer Credit Counseling Service and signed onto their program to pay off all her bills.

It took several years for her to get out of debt. She was actually able to complete the program faster than expected, because as a part of taking responsibility for her creations she also began to learn that honesty was equally as important as good credit! In all the years that she was spending out of control, she was living a lie. The breaking point came after this last divorce. She was introduced to a guy named David. He came from a fairly wealthy family and had a bunch of money himself. He was a cutie–patooty and was also into having fun, but he was a "high roller." She bought $400 dresses to impress him. She charged plane tickets to Europe and Jackson Hole and went on expensive vacations with him that she couldn't afford.

She wasn't being honest with others and certainly was not honest with herself. Who did she think she was fooling? Hand in hand with setting a strict budget to retire the debt was the commitment to complete honesty. This was another major turning point in her life.

Chapter Seven
Soul Mate

In her mid–forties, Jean met her soul mate. Had she not been so eager to find love and be married earlier, she would have waited for him. The Universal Law of Correspondence says that as soon as we desire something, the object of our desire is right next to the desire in the Universal Mind. So, if we let go and let God, and put emotion behind our request and believe we have it, we receive what we desire. If we doubt or yearn, we push the object further away. Therefore, what she wanted so badly, she pushed farther out.

Her husband is the Solid Rock that relationships can build upon. He has the patience of Job, and has stood by her through meteoric spiritual growth in the last twelve years. They met when she was working on her Theology degree, still wrapped up in the traditional Christian environment. Unknowingly, they shared mutual friends, Diane and Cheryl. These women worked with Jean, but Cheryl had dated Larry years before and Diane had been his sales rep. One day, they compared notes and decided Jean was the "female version of their buddy, Larry." They began chatting each up individually, trying to set up a match. Larry was agreeable, but Jean was fed up with men – she was tired of their letting her down. Eventually, Diane and Cheryl got their way, and the match was made. They were right! Jean was the female version of Larry. He had skipped a grade in grammar school, and started college at sixteen. They had similar tastes in music; both had played in a band. They each had three unsuccessful marriages under their belts, with three similar scenarios: married too young to one, another with an addictive personality and the third mentally unbalanced! Before long, they were finishing each other's sentences.

Larry was the first person she was ever totally honest with. When she shared her financial problem with him, her FINAL husband, he offered to help her repay the debt quickly. In every story there is a lesson, and while the debt story taught her the Law of Cause and Effect in a big way, she might not have seen her issues with honesty any other way. There is a fine line between doing everything ourselves and accepting assistance when we need it. Larry's offering to bail her out, and her allowing him to help was a major healing step. It allowed that glimpse of unconditional love to reappear. He didn't judge her for the mess she had created.

Metaphysically money is energy and love is energy, therefore, in this instance money equaled love in a way that our little girl had been trying to make happen but never was able to. She'd gotten caught up in the illusion of looking at money as "stuff" and "stuff" as love and it wasn't the same. What she didn't understand is that money is actually the reflection of love and not love itself.

There are NO accidents, and everything happens as it is supposed to and for a reason. We all co–create all the family and relationship situations in our lives. We choose our family, our relationships, and all the drama we create. This is not about victim mentality at any level. Jean picked her Dad to facilitate his clearing with his father's soul. She picked her Mom to learn about giving away power. She chose both of them to teach her about definition, finding her boundaries. As it has turned out, they did pretty much what they signed up to do. She picked each of her husbands for the lessons they offered, as well.

Larry has watched with a raised eyebrow as she completed her studies then moved into metaphysics and healing, but his support has never wavered. Jean praises God every day for bringing him into her life! Everything has not been "roses" in their time together, because as the Course says, "love brings up everything unlike itself for the purpose of healing and release." They have helped each other heal and grow considerably – and they are still working on it.

For example, she had never balanced a checkbook. It never seemed important, but she always recorded the checks she wrote and verified each bank statement to make sure they deducted the proper amount. Larry always analyzed every decision, down to creating spreadsheets before making a purchase, no matter how small. He has taught her how to properly balance a checkbook and she has started to show him that God will supply all our needs. It's a pretty fair trade!

Results prove whether or not something is working. Larry has been quite skeptical of her work, particularly where it diverges from his Christian heritage (which was even more fundamental than hers). He began to question her sanity and her "salvation" when she started mentioning past lives or clearing forces from long dead ancestors – especially clearing forces from her deceased parents. He really lost it when she told him that she'd done a session that showed that she was the reincarnation of her paternal grandfather!

But the truth remains; he sees that she is not the needy woman he originally met. He also reluctantly sees that when she trusts God to supply whatever she needs, it happens. Part of her growth process has been to show her, not so delicately I might add, that she can't help Larry to believe like she does. We can't change anyone, we can only live our life as our authentic self and teach by example.

She has certainly tried to change Larry, among others, and the results have not been pretty.

Gradually, though, he is becoming more in tune with what she's learning, with living in concert with the Universal Laws. Recently he took part in the first evening of a seminar she was hosting at their home. The Friday night part was an intro with a meditation. Larry had never done a guided meditation before, but thought, "what the heck – it's free!" In the midst of the meditation, he told Jean later, "It felt like a rod had been pressed through the top of my head and down my spine. It started shaking at my tailbone and the shaking moved all the way up my back and out the top of my head. It scared the shit out of me!" She laughed and replied, "That's unreal! There are folks that work their entire life to achieve what you received without even asking! What happened to you is called Kundalini Rising, and it's all about the opening of your chakras and the raising of your consciousness. I'm jealous!"

Larry doesn't want Jean "inside his head". He's a very private person, so, like many, he is leery of the InnerSpeak process, which really opens up one's Soul to talk about what is blocking it and keeping one from achieving full potential. He has seen that the process eliminates conscious control by using hand positions and muscle testing. He doesn't like giving up control! InnerSpeak gets the conscious mind out of the way, bypassing the chatter, interference, and rationalization that keeps us stuck in familiar, if unhealthy patterns. Larry is very comfortable with Reiki, however. As soon as he realized that Reiki relieved pain, he was sold on it. He's even been overheard telling other people how well it works! He's received his first two attunements and works on himself quite a bit, so he is where he is supposed to be.

Larry gets the most credit, however, for not running away when Jean lost her corporate job and moved into service work. They had talked a lot early on in their relationship about ambition and work ethic. He had been married three times before, twice to women who really didn't want to work, so one of his "criteria" was a wife who wanted to work. The disconnect that happened was that in their discussions, they never really defined what "work" looked like.

He had never considered that her work might be metaphysical healing and helping others to find their path! To Larry, what Jean considered to be her work and her passion looked like "retirement" to him.

There have been some painful times around this. Jean wanted to please both of them, and the lesson she learned from this is the impossibility of doing that. In order for her to "please" Larry, she was slipping away from the commitment of total honesty that they had based their relationship on. She was once again not being honest with herself! As she minimized her mission and tried to act the way she thought he expected her to, she was not acting out of integrity and it began to take a toll on her physically. In the scriptures, when Jesus said, "you can not serve God and mammon," this is exactly what he was talking about. In trying to serve her Higher Self and Larry at the same time, she was failing both miserably.

She had reached a turning point in her life. She'd been studying healing work in her spare time and actually had learned several modalities. She had begun to see positive results on the people that let her work on them. She was gaining a sense of satisfaction, no more than that, she felt blessed. She was being allowed to be present while miracles were happening. For the first time in her life she clearly knew what she was here to do and felt passionately that she wanted to dedicate the rest of her life to healing others and herself. Unfortunately, she had that very well paying career in sales. The largest conflict of her life was staring her in the face. A choice had to be made, one that was going to alter the course of her life forever. She manifested two "biggies" from this decision – severe foot pain, ala plantar fasciatis, and the bankruptcy of the company she was employed by as a Regional Sales Manager.

A most interesting session came out of that foot pain. It was so severe that she could hardly walk, so she began doing sessions to find out why, and up popped her grandfather to heal the pain from his lifetime. These sessions showed that she was his reincarnation. This was so far out of the realm of Jean's comprehension that she immediately found a hypnotherapist to verify this. When she was regressed under hypnosis, the session's findings were confirmed. Her soul and the soul of her paternal grandfather were one and the same. Since he died five years before she was born, she never had the opportunity to know him, obviously.

Her paternal grandmother crossed over shortly after him, so other than her Dad and his siblings, she got little information about either one of them while she was growing up. In fact, she was never really close to John's side of the family and had a strained relationship with her father until his death – which was when she found out that he had actually disinherited her!

What came out of the sessions that followed painted a picture that showed that Jacob, her grandfather, was a very unhappy and troubled man, who had emotionally disconnected from others. He cynically distrusted others' motives and had lost faith in himself by the time he passed. What she found could only be described as coldness, unfeeling and unmerciful. Jacob dealt with many issues –

lack of education made it hard for him to find fulfilling work. He had a succession of jobs, and sometime around the Great Depression, after moving his family several times in order to find work, he developed a problem with alcohol. Perhaps because that lifetime was so close to her present one, it weighed her down much of her life, but as she began to develop a strong passion for what she wanted to become and do, this energy attachment from the prior reincarnation grew stronger, causing her to lose faith in herself and shut off inflows of information from her higher self, teachers and guides. The pain in her feet made it difficult for her to pursue her goals – ANY GOALS! She could not walk her path because she literally could not walk! While all this was going on internally, externally there she was, embroiled in a conflict about moving forward with this new career choice and starting from financial zero, or pleasing her husband by finding another $150,000/year job in sales. It was not until she decided to "take a stand" and actually declare that she was going to dedicate her energy to her new healing work, and give it a chance that the foot pain went away. She finally stood up for her truth and began to move forward on her path.

The next physical problem was with her right knee, which developed a painful and almost crippling problem, a torn cartilage from an accidental encounter with her ninety–pound Doberman, Crissy. Sessions showed this stemmed from not making the right choices in life. At some point in his life, her grandfather, Jacob, fell and injured his knee, creating the force. Periodically when she's faced with self–imposed blocks, either to her creativity or her spirituality, she will have bouts with severe knee pain – reminders of "stuff" she brought in from that lifetime. Over the years, she's had a series of throat infections that sessions showed were about not speaking her truth. But most of all, she just wasn't happy.

The biggest physical implication that happened during their relationship, though, has had to do with weight. Weight issues have plagued Jean through out her life, but for the most part, after her first divorce and the move to Atlanta, she'd managed to keep it under control. While she was never "skinny," she was quite attractive, trim and fit between the ages of 28 and 45, maintaining her weight within about 5 pounds of flux.

About the time she stepped on her spiritual path, she began to put on weight. From a medical perspective, the cause was Graves disease, an autoimmune problem that causes the thyroid to turn on itself and produce massive amounts of thyroid hormone. The majority of people that get this problem lose large quantities of weight for no apparent reason, but a small percentage of women in Jean's age bracket gain. Of course, she would have to be one of the "lucky" ones! From a metaphysical perspective, thyroid disease is caused by the belief that "I can't have what I want when I want it." At the same time that she was growing spiritually, she was also in conflict with Larry about getting married. They'd been living together for what Jean considered to be long enough, they had discussed marriage and knew that it would be the ultimate outcome, and Jean was READY. Unfortunately, Larry had put on brakes! He liked the way their relationship was, and since he'd had a couple of disastrous marriages where the women turned out not to be who he thought they were, he didn't want to take the chance that it would happen again. Bottom line? She put on one hundred pounds in ten years!

From a metaphysical standpoint, she knew that weight was about fear, and that we put on weight as protection. Sounds good.

What exactly did she have to be afraid of? She had a good life, a man she loved, good job, great kids, cool dog, nice house and stuff – lots of stuff. It didn't make sense. She began to do sessions on it.

In the beginning, she found all those ancestors and cleared their fears. That took at least a year. Then she started working on past lives. For some reason, more important issues kept coming up as she was clearing past lives, issues that distracted her from working on her weight. So, she'd leave the weight problem for a while, months sometimes, while she dealt with whatever seemed to be more pressing at the time. She'd have times where she'd get results and would lose weight – eighty pounds one time, and was back within reaching distance of where she was when it began coming on, but inevitably the pounds would return. Eventually, she stopped working on it completely.

She was beginning to find that she really loved herself, and decided that unconditional love meant that she should love herself just the way she was, overweight and all. She knew, REALLY KNEW, that deep down inside the fat was a truly lovable person, so it had to be ok.

The truth is that with a couple of exceptions, it is ok. Unfortunately, being one hundred pounds overweight is not healthy. The weight was not serving her because the vessel that houses her lovable, wonderful Inner was beginning to have even more physical issues: heart palpitations, lack of stamina and joint pain. The other major stumbling block has to do with the delivery of her message. As a healer with an important message to tell, how believable can the message be if her body, which is her creation, doesn't reflect her message? Here's the paradox – she continually tells her clients to judge their work by their results. If the results reflect the outcome you expect then you are doing the right thing. If they don't, then you'd better re–examine what you are doing. It was time for her to look carefully at what she was doing relative to her own vessel! It was time for her to let go of the armor and trust in God to protect her, just like she trusts God to supply.

She started doing sessions on her weight again. In the meantime, she'd cleared away enough extraneous gunk that the forces surrounding the weight were right there for releasing. The truth is that everything happens when it's supposed to, so it was finally time. Now, what she was finding was that the fear was about her power. In too many lifetimes, she'd hurt other people with her power. Too many of her ancestors had done the same thing, and she carried their forces as well. She was afraid that to claim her power would mean making the same mistakes all over again.

There was more to it than that. Her biggest fear revolved around what might happen to her marriage if Larry were able to see how powerful she really was. She had placed one hundred pounds of armor around her power so that no one, especially Larry, would know it was there. It took two months of digging and struggling to let go of all the fear around that. The biggest help during that time came from three of her terrific friends who are able to "see" things. Patricia, the friend who does the DNA activations along with other very powerful healing work, traded sessions with her one day.

At the end of the session she told Jean that she had "seen" the real Jean and that she was TINY! Another of her psychic friends, Julia, told her in passing that when she looked at her she saw a very thin woman. The third confirmation was from Cherie.

Cherie is a long time client. In the beginning, Jean would go to client's homes to do sessions. She became particularly fond of Cherie's animals... They connected, and she practiced her animal communication skills on them from time to time. Cherie's cat, Hobbes passed over quite suddenly. She called Jean in distress, wanting her to "talk" to him to find out what happened. Jean and Cherie talked for a long time and she tried her best to console her. Some time later Cherie asked Jean, "Did you come to me in the middle of the night to comfort me?" Jean was taken aback by the question, because she has no clue where she "goes" when she's sleeping. Cherie said, "I saw you clearly in my living room, just as if you were standing there. The only thing that was different was that you were tiny, you were skinny!" Knowing that three women she trusted could see the "real Jean," even though she wasn't able to at the time, gave her the strength and the belief that she could actually lose the weight and achieve what they were seeing!

When she finally processed through the denial in enough sessions and realized what was happening, she was able to return to a space of honesty in her relationship with Larry. She stated firmly that she had no plans to return to the corporate world, that she was called to do the healing work and teach others how to do it. She told him how she felt when he made sarcastic remarks about her "getting a day job." She told him in no uncertain terms how much their relationship and he specifically meant to her. She told him that she would never leave, and though she would certainly continue to change and grow, change did not mean abandonment. Amazing things began to happen! The physical ailments went away one by one. Their relationship began to bloom once more. Who did she think she'd been fooling, once again? Larry had known all along that something wasn't right. It was actually a relief for her to "come out" with how strong her convictions about her work were. And, guess what? He didn't leave! As time has passed, he is even beginning to understand her spirituality. There are times when he can explain her work better than she can!

What Larry has been able to show that is so important, is unconditional love. Before she met him, the only time she had experienced this was the immature version received from the high school boyfriend or the deep love that was received from Aunt Lil and Granny. Growing up, she spent almost every weekend with one or the other; from the time she was five or six years old. They cultivated her creativity, let her explore freely and did not criticize. She received the unconditional love in their homes that was missing in her own.

This is how the Plan B life contract played out. John and Mildred did love her, no doubt, but they behaved in patterns that they learned from their individual upbringings. They did the best they knew how, but both of them had issues with intimacy and expressing love. These were some of the main lessons that Jean's soul had elected to work on, and as dysfunctional as their family was, it was the perfect place to do it. As an adult, Jean had never found unconditional love from any member of the opposite sex. Once again, like the Course so aptly points out, this brought up everything unlike itself for healing and release. Before Larry and Jean got married, she ended up in several years of psychotherapy because she didn't know how to handle this level of love. Through therapy and InnerSpeak sessions, she's been able to clear enough of her childhood, past life and ancestral trauma to enable her to function at a much higher level and stay in a rewarding relationship with her husband, and this is a very good thing.

Part III
Sparks of God: Souls Never Die

Chapter Eight
Expanding Beliefs

This part of the story started with the "Big Bang", when souls were individualized – billions of years ago. The soul never dies. Each of our souls was created then as a "spark" of God and has been in existence ever since. Just our form has changed over time. Some of us have spent more time in physical form than others, but that doesn't mean any of us is better than another, perhaps just more "experienced."

Until I was in my forties, I had never really given it much thought. My upbringing this time around was in a fundamental Christian family. There was no mention of reincarnation, or if it was brought up it was dismissed as heresy. Consequently, I felt a lot of conflict when I began studying healing work and began to see what seemed to be consistent evidence that we have been here before. This wasn't the first time that I had doubted the things I had been taught. Perhaps because of the Father/God issues I had from my childhood, I spent many years studying religions – Western and Eastern – Protestant and Roman Catholic Christian, Mormon, Hindu, Islam, Pagan – looking for answers to questions I didn't even know. I just wanted to understand who this "Father/God" was and to find out what I needed to do to earn His approval and love. It was important to me to find the Truth, and it seems that the Truth is a combination of pieces of all of them.

Each of the dogmas I studied is "right." God is the same God, regardless of what He/She is called. It's a single Source, and each of our souls is a clone of that One Source. Within each of us lies the spark of the Divine and the knowledge of All That Is and all that has ever been. It is up to each one of us to awaken that sleeping knowledge and recover that Divine Spark in order to walk his/her path to enlightenment and completion of the life mission that was committed to by us before our descent to the physical plane. In order to achieve this, we have to strip away layers upon layers of learned behavior and fear.

Evidence becomes *evidence* as one begins to see it as such. My first healing sessions were focused on my experiences with kindred souls and how their issues were causing problems in my life. Then came the ancestors – and boy, did they come. It was as though they realized, after a few sessions, that I was willing to be a surrogate for them to facilitate the removal of their pain and the traumas that occured during their lives. It was as if they were standing in line for help! For almost a year, I would work on "whoever needs it today." There were several women from my deep ancestral past who lost children in childbirth or infancy from disease, setting painful belief structures and constructs that haunted them throughout their lives. There were men who carried great guilt from killing others in wars. There were women who were abandoned or cheated on, that passed on feelings of no worth down through the lineage.

My reality, up to this point in my life, didn't contain any basis for looking at sources of pain outside what I could personally remember. The dead were dead, gone from this plane of existence and not able to impact my life. Wrong! As my beliefs began to expand and as I was able to release the fears that limited my vision of the world, past lives began to present themselves for clearing, both for me and for my clients, as well.

Chapter Nine
The Lightbearer

Every generation of each family branch has one member that is designated as the "lightbearer." This soul is the one who is able to bring forward forces for clearing on behalf of the ancestors of this lineage. It is an awesome responsibility, which can become burdensome, but avails the one with this "honor" of terrific rewards and healing opportunities. The beauty of this process is that when one clears for an ancestor, all the remaining members of the line are healed at the same instant! For example, when I heal for someone on my dad's side 15 generations back, I am blessed with the knowledge that neither my brother, nor his children, nor my own children or grandchildren yet to come have to deal with that particular force.

The lightbearer is the brother, sister, or cousin who everyone else in the family thinks is a little "nutty." They generally appear to be the one with all the issues, and why wouldn't they? They carry the issues of all the generations of ancestors before them. In my work as a healing facilitator, they are easy to spot. This individual will generally be a client who returns for many sessions, and usually clears for an ancestor while they are clearing for themselves. It is my belief that the soul volunteers for, or agrees to, this job prior to returning to the physical plane.

Our ancestral identities are held within our bodies at the cellular level, and when a crisis in our life stimulates these stored memories, the ancestor "wakes up" and becomes very present in our life, changing it to the point that we become uncomfortable or blocked in some way. There are many "signals" that this has happened: anger rages out of control, illness pops up, sexual or relationship problems develop, creativity becomes blocked, and our self–confidence dims.

This lightbearing is not just limited to clearing forces for ancestors. There are many metafields that welcome assistance in healing inner pain. Some of us are here with the capability of clearing for groups – cultures, races, genders and even nations. Some of us clear for members of our Soul Group, or our affinity network. Some lightbearers clear for the entire human race, and the circle of possibilities grows larger and larger, as far as the mind can conceive.

The first sessions I had done on myself were lightbearing sessions. Initially I found that I could assist an affinity net member in healing while positively affecting my own reality. Next, I found that there were also many ancestors who had crossed over with hidden trauma and inner pain. I knew that it was my duty to step forward in surrendering to God and make myself available as the tool to lift these forces away... not just for the ancestor, but to heal my own inner pain as well.

Much of the ancestral hurt on my father's side of the family appears to revolve around walling off of their feelings, blaming others, and shutting away inner guidance. A common thread seems to be a deeply held belief that "I can never get what I want." Some of the earliest ancestral information from my dad's side dates back as far as 200BC, where an insatiable hungering for the Truth interfered with the ability of a female ancestor to "hear" the voice of God. This left her feeling very alone, setting up the mistaken thought that "I must defend myself because God isn't." These two deeply held beliefs have been very detrimental in my life, and I have to believe this misinformation has been damaging in my family for centuries, even though I've only been able to find a relatively small portion of my ancestral population in sessions. They seem to set up a self–fulfilling prophecy, attempting to excuse destructive behavior, while living it out in their life. When they die without resolving the issue(s), it appears to get coded genetically and passed on down the line. Remember the biblical scripture about the sins of the father being visited on the sons, even to the seventh generation? Well, from these sessions it seems that it doesn't stop at seven generations. We can carry forces from very deep ancestry – twenty or more generations back!

Early in the 700's in South America a woman ancestor in my Dad's lineage lost her unborn child due to physical abuse from her husband. She was beaten and kicked and the child was stillborn. This set up a deep, unmoving sadness within her, erasing the urge to survive and experience the joy of life. This same ancestor came up in a later session, when I was working on building up my healing business. At this time a new facet of the force appeared – this woman kept a belief that all men are animals and she shut down her second chakra, which has to do with sexual, financial, creative abilities and issues. This block has permeated my entire paternal lineage, showing up most recently in both my father and grandfather.

These forces appear to have congealed into a generalized feeling of being wrong and not being able to do anything about it by the 1100's. The earlier family issues distorted emotional clarity and raised problems with authority, both my ancestor's authority and the ability to deal with the authority of others. Again, it is important to remember that the soul chooses when and where to return to work on releasing the attachment to fear and moving through its mission in love. Therefore, it only makes sense that my soul's path would resonate with the issues in my father's line!

In the early 1200's, there was a male ancestor on Daddy's side who appeared in a session for clearing. This man held many of the beliefs just discussed, as well as a deep hungering for love and a difficulty in pursuing his goals. Does this sound familiar? He lost faith in himself, causing his intentions to become inverted (I want, I can't have – I don't want, I get). His impact on my life was two–fold. I was having difficulty getting new clients for my business, but the true importance here is that this ancestor is reincarnated, living now – my husband! So, in clearing for this ancestor, I was not only helping myself but also healing a part of my husband's karmic contract for this incarnation. Almost immediately after this session, my ability to manifest clients shifted. The next week, my schedule was fuller than it had been since I started doing healing work. The shift in Larry was perceptible, too. He became more focused in the pursuit of his goals, restoring his faith in himself and his ability to succeed. For over a year he had been involved in a project that kept getting bogged down. He had fallen into the trap of believing that it was his fault. Once his perspective was restored, his efforts became more productive. When he shifted, the energy of his team shifted and the project took on a new life. I'm constantly amazed at how connected we all are. When one of us heals, we all heal in some way.

In a later session, this man came up again – bringing up a basic meaning for existence that needed to be examined for both my husband and myself – Unconditional Love. I am sure that is the reason that Larry and I have come together in this life. This ancestor, however, didn't really understand the Universal Laws of

Choice and Action. We always have a choice. We can choose how we want to allow a situation to affect us, and we can choose how we want to react to anything that occurs around us. This man apparently blamed and hated others for his inability to succeed. What we send out to others returns to us, so his hopes were further crushed as these thoughts returned back to him.

At about this same time period in my life, there appeared a man in my mother's ancestry who has shown quite a bit of control on my inner reality, causing me to have difficulties in pursuit of my goals because of fear of stepping into the unknown. Why this ancestor lost his courage never became clear in session, but this old consciousness has certainly had the effect of blocking my ability to hear my inner guidance until this man was helped to go into the Light.

This brings up an interesting point about ancestral forces – it seems that in most cases these ancestors just don't realize that they have crossed over! Their negative influence is quickly lifted by visualization exercises that assist them in reaching the light and moving on to a higher plane of existence. Fear is the largest stumbling block I've seen. Due to whatever crisis that happened to the ancestor during their life, they seem to be afraid to make the paradigm shift to the other side. Some are afraid of repercussions for their wrong doings. Some just aren't sure that there is really another place that they should go to. They are SO grateful when they are helped to move on – they freely repay their "assistant" with increased abilities and other gifts. Some of the blessings you get for helping them out include, good luck, increased psychic abilities, courage, and synchronicity or the ability to have your life flow smoothly. It's as though these ancestors have no idea how painful and disruptive their influence can be when they call out to those of us on the physical plane to help them. They don't realize that their cry for help causes physical and emotional pain to the person that hears it, and when they "get" that in session, they seem to really want to make it up to their helper.

The second maternal ancestor I cleared also had the effect of blocking me on my path. His life crisis had to do with misuse of power, and the genetic coding from this, that was passed on placed openness to perceptive abilities under a pall of unease – good old fear strikes again! From this I inherited a block of the third eye chakra. All my life, for as far back as I can remember, I have wanted to be psychic. Somewhere in my teens, when I learned about astrology, I read that Pisces was one of the most psychic signs. I tried everything to "find" my ability that should have been my birthright, according to the horoscope books. I stared into candles, used the Ouiji Board, and bought all sorts of oracle games, all to no discernable avail.

The misuse of the power force from this session was part of the block I was experiencing, and when this ancestor was cleared and allowed to move on, it was also a part of restoring my psychic abilities. The true block to my third eye was the fear of doing what he did, misusing my power. Lifetime after lifetime in my own incarnations I've dealt with this as well, like what happened early on in my healing career.

I was working on a client and the session led to having her access her Akashic records from a previous life, where she'd rejected the soul that is now her husband, along with the souls that are now her stepchildren. She quickly found the records and was able to see the error of her ways. Without thinking or asking whether or not this was in her highest and best good, I told her to re–write the records to have the situation turn out as she would have like it to. Sounds innocent enough, right? Not! She called me two days later, in tears and said, "I don't know what we did in session the other day, but my life has gone from bad to worse – I'm miserable, I want out of my marriage. This certainly is not what I wanted when we were working on that lifetime!" Immediately, a sense of dread came over me and I knew exactly what I had done. I told her that I'd call her back in just a few minutes. As soon as I hung up the phone, I heard the voice of the Archangel Metatron, who is the keeper of the Akashic records, saying, "This is what you all did that cost you a continent in the days of Atlantis!" I was mortified and asked if the situation could be corrected. He cleared what had been done, and thankfully, this woman's life has been restored to normal. Never again will I mess with something that's not mine to touch, and never will I let my ego self "drive."

In about the same timeframe lived a female ancestor who had the same influence – blocking knowledge and my ability to create out of inspiration, as well as making it hard for me to truly surrender my will to God's direction. Her life's pain came from denied infidelity. This has manifested for me in not being honest with others and myself as I've already shown. When we are able to follow the direction of Spirit, claiming our integrity and living it, knowledge and creative inspiration flow freely. She was another step in finding my authentic self and living my truth. For almost a year, my father's grandmother presented herself for clearing. It's probably safe to say that of all the ancestors and past lives I've cleared, she has had the most profound influence. I did around twenty–five sessions on helping her. Of course, she did have some major crises in her life. She married a physician who already had one son. They, then, had two children of their own.

When their oldest, my grandmother, was about eight, a baby was left on the doorstep of their home with a note attached proclaiming the child to be my great–grandfather's son. This devastated my great–grandmother, and she took their two children and left that day, moving home to her mother, never to return. She died with unresolved issues of betrayal, intimacy, feelings of not being attractive, and being ignored by God, and the list goes on and on. I certainly have shared all of them.

It is also interesting to note here that recently, my great–grandfather presented himself for the first time for healing. His issue was a broken heart, and his contribution to me was an inappropriate model of authority, along with a wealth of sadness and the inability to find the love I desired. It was lovely to be able to gain clarity on both sides of that situation, because it had never occurred to me that he was anything other than a philandering jerk! In the Bible, Jesus said, "Judge not, that ye be not judged." This is the Universal Law of No Judgments, and breaking this law sets up scenarios where the judgment turns on us in ways we can't anticipate. We never truly know what is in the heart of another, despite appearances, therefore, walking in surrender means knowing that mistakes occur and loving despite them.

Because of my great–grandfather's mistake, he lost his beloved family. In fact, my paternal grandmother never saw him again – because each time he would try to visit her she would refuse. In those days and in that particular area of north Florida, fathers generally got custody of the girls and mothers got custody of the boys. My grandmother lived in fear that her father would "take her away" from her mother, so she refused his contact. In doing so she set up the force of not being able to have a positive love relationship with one's father.

Another woman on my mother's side of the family, eight generations back, dealt with the pain of physical abuse, which stifled her ability to stand up for herself. This genetic coding has caused me to feel "I'd rather switch than fight" – a recurring pattern of compromise and running from confrontation rather than taking a stand. This is another source of my not honoring my truth and having such deep–seated issues with honesty. This stuck perspective on creative expression also shuts off inspiration. No wonder it's taken me so long to realize that I could actually write a book!!

At this point, I began to see another ancestral pattern emerging – victim mentality, wounded power centers, power given away and distracted from life's purpose. These inner wounds have been deeply hidden, but passed on from generation to generation in the women of my mother's lineage. Over and over, sessions with my maternal ancestors repeated beliefs of "I can't do anything about it", isolation and shame. Repeatedly, there were incarnations filled with abusiveness and cruelty that caused these women to shut away their own true identities, all the while shutting away their inner guidance and the still, small voice of God. How lonely I have been in this lifetime – how lonely they must have also been.

From the men in my mother's and my father's lines, I found another different but no less destructive pattern – intimacy issues with others and with God. When you couple a line of women who have loneliness and isolation issues with a line of men who have intimacy problems, it's not surprising to find such struggle! The little girl who just wanted to be loved chose the perfect environment to come into to learn very powerful lessons.

My maternal grandmother, Granny, dealt with many of these forces. When she was very young, she was "spotted" by the man that would later become my grandfather, Arthur. He was fifteen or so years her senior, but vowed he would wait for her to grow up. He pursued her ardently and they married when she reached eighteen. They had four daughters – Mildred, Lil and twins, Florene and Lorene. Arthur died when the twins were less than two. She taught school to make ends meet and Mil and Lil, each took responsibility for one of the twins. Granny never remarried – as far as I know, she never even dated anyone. She lost the one man she ever loved and spent the rest of her life in struggle. She's returned to the earth plane to work through many of these lessons. In session after session, my daughter, Amanda, deals with her past life issues of, loss of love and struggle. Amanda's last incarnation was Granny!

Another session cleared a coping mechanism that had severely damaged my second chakra and was set up apparently by my Dad this time around, almost forcing me to reincarnate as his child to clear pain caused from his own lifetime and his less than perfect relationship with his father (me.) This sourcing in the InnerSpeak process is called "Plan B Contracts" and implies that while there are no accidents, especially with respect to choosing a lifetime and a mission, sometimes a desire can subconsciously be so strong as to rearrange priorities.

So the program that I accepted at incarnation was all about allowing others to control me through dependency, self–sabotage and the inability to see the big picture in order to coordinate my outer world with my inner need for true freedom. I have attempted to wall off this trauma by taking on addictions to food and to excessive spending, among other things. I've created a lot of struggle for myself through violation of the Laws of Flexibility and Choices by not standing firm with what I knew I should be doing; the Law of Patterns, by taking on addictions to mask inner pain and the Law of Action by not moving forward and taking action immediately when I found my true calling.

In the last few weeks, my paternal grandmother has presented herself for healing. I knew something was up, because I had started putting on weight and my inflow of money seemed to be blocked. Additionally, I appeared to be attracting clients who were unwilling to take responsibility for their own healing, even after their sessions were complete. In a series of several sessions on myself, Florrie came in loud and clear. She was ready to confront her husband, Jake (now me) for the lack of love she had received when they were married. She was also really angry about his inability to be "present" and sensitive to her needs. She resented his lack of education and initiative. Through the session, we released her anger and bitterness. The visualization of Florrie and Jake forgiving each other was a particularly emotional event for me.

Chapter Ten
The Long Path—Many Lifetimes

When I was able to cut a path through the ancestors who had "raised their hands" for help, I began to have sessions that related to past lives of my own. That put me into a tailspin. It brought up my belief system for examination. At first, I denied the possibility that I had been here before, figuring that it must be imagination. I would take classes and folks would suggest that I read books on reincarnation. I'd decline, saying, "I'm just not sure I believe in that." Our conscious mind/ego is quite creative in blocking out anything that it really doesn't want to deal with, especially when dealing with those issues brings up feelings of fear.

We go through paradigm shifts and move through differing dimensional realities, but the soul stays constant. It is my belief that as the soul moves, it chooses to make these shifts and, as it decides to take on a physical shape and exist in form, to learn a lesson, or serve a particular purpose or experience what can only be experienced in a body, the soul forms a plan of what it should be or do during that incarnation. This takes place while the soul exists on the Spiritual plane, and at the time of incarnation, the memories of that mission, the Spiritual plane and previous lives and lessons, all are erased from the mind of the child about to be born. The memories are erased from the mind, but remain within the Soul, the "Inner", and they color the very existence of the person that child becomes. The struggle that the Soul must go through, the battle that must be overcome, is to move through the new lifetime and its mission in Love, not in Fear.

Fear is the unique "gotcha" of the reality of the body. It is the creation of the physical plane and the primary obstacle that we are here to overcome. Fear is the singular block to our reaching the heights and obtaining all the blessings that are waiting to be poured out onto us. Fear has many faces – anger, resentment, jealousy, judgment, disappointment, sadness, illness. In fact, all forces are a form of fear. *A Course In Miracles* states that anything that is not love is fear.

Eventually, enough past life sessions got "in my face" so that the evidence was strong enough that I had to believe that there must be something to it. Now, after facilitating sessions on clients for several years, I know and accept that it must be so. There was too much evidence for it to just be coincidental!

It is my goal that these stories will help others to open up to their own beliefs around reincarnation and not have to face the conflict that I did. Maybe then each person can uncover the untold mysteries in their own life. Most Eastern religions include karma and reincarnation as part of their dogma. At one time, probably the Hebrew religion did as well, but the translation that has come down through the ages as Christianity has omitted those teachings. I have poured over the Holy Bible, trying to find references that exclude it from Christian doctrine without success. What I have found, however, is at least one example that would seem to support it. In the New Testament, John the Baptist is referred to as the prophet Elijah returned.

The earliest documentation of the existence of my soul came in an InnerSpeak session. That "lifetime" was so far back that it seems that it was before we began incarnating into bodies on the physical plane. At that time, my soul and the soul of my mother in this life-time were together. We did not get along – it would appear that the stage was set for this lifetime way back then! Her soul was very judgmental of mine, jealous perhaps. The remnants of the pain felt by my soul put what was probably the first "brick" into the wall of defensiveness that has concealed my true being for eons to come. This wall has been hiding me from my own pure potential since that time.

Medicine has documented that the physical body heals top down, inside out and latest symptom or problem first, oldest last. The InnerSpeak process doesn't appear to work that way. One's Inner, or soul, chooses to remove the "brick" that has the highest priority in the process of helping the soul to achieve its mission for this lifetime. When enough bricks are taken away, the wall tumbles down, opening the path for the soul to see clearly what it came here to accomplish and how to reach that goal. The following lifetimes of my own soul are documented not in the order that the sessions took place, but chronologically according to the times of the incar-nations. These memory "tracings" come to the surface in many ways. They may be activated by a crisis (illness, automobile acci-dent, argument, rejection) that will awaken the memory and feel-ings of all the similar crises the soul has ever experienced. These inner memories then take over our outer world and we find our-selves acting out scenarios that bleach the happiness from our exis-tence. Sometimes we actually incarnate with the trauma being active, in which case our entire life is colored by what has hap-pened before.

Female, Mediterranean Area, Prior to 50,000BC

I believe that the human species was seeded on this planet, created by beings, or "Gods" from outside our solar system, to be servants – miners and otherwise to these beings. The human species was not supposed to be able to procreate. In this very early lifetime, I was a servant. I fell in love with another servant and somehow conceived and gave birth to twins that I attempted to hide in my hut. The souls of these twins have been with me as I have incarnated in many lifetimes, but most currently, these souls are in my life as my two children, Rob and Amanda. The soul of their father, my soul mate, is with me now, Larry. The "Gods" found the twins and took them away. They took my lover away and killed him. My vision of this showed that this was handled in a very cavalier manner, and I was devastated. This is the earliest instance I have found where my soul totally felt the separation from God and the resultant pain. This lifetime set up a belief that "if I give birth to something, I will lose everything I love." It should come as no surprise that this lifetime showed up in a session while I was struggling to give birth to this book! Another thing that happened to precipitate my doing the session that brought up this lifetime for clearing was the death of my daughter–in–law's younger brother. I hardly knew him, met him at their wedding, but when he was killed in a wreck, it was very traumatic for me. It brought up the memory of my own children being taken away from me for no reason, and the devastating feeling of losing what I loved that I had felt thousands of years and thousands of lifetimes ago.

Several Lifetimes as Women in Egypt, Between 6000 BC and 1500BC

The earliest of the Egyptian lifetimes was actually found in a session I was doing on a client. She has my mother in that incarnation! We were among the last of the line of Nefertiti, carrying the physical structure of elongated heads, two hearts, and being extremely tall. These beings were known as the "Sons of God" and were descended from the Nefilim, the extra–terrestrial race that created humanity on the planet. They had many gifts – the ability to read minds and communicate telepathically among them. My mother was killed at my birth. The twelve men that attended the birth placed a leather strap over her third eye so that her gifts would not be passed on to me and then cut her belly open with a sharpened rock to remove me.

This was done to dishonor her, because they had advanced medical skills at that time and could have delivered the baby without taking the life of the mother, had they so desired. Because that was the level of race consciousness belief, I did not inherit her gifts. Soon after, the genetic traits of the Sons of God disappeared from the earth. Basically, what this means to me is that I probably have had tremendous abilities at the soul level, but they were shut down as far back as this lifetime!

I found the next Egyptian incarnation during the time I was writing the InnerSpeak Process manual. I was struggling with my decision to break away from the man that had taught me his method of clinical kinesiology. I was afraid of his reaction when he found out that I was heading off in a different direction, so I was secretive about what I was doing, sharing my discoveries and insights with only a few close friends. In that life, I was a candidate for initiation in the Great Pyramid. My teacher was jealous of my knowledge and skills. I think he believed that if I should succeed at the Initiation, I would become more powerful than he was. Under the pretext of telling me how to pass the tests, he lied. I failed and drowned in a pool of crocodiles.

This man is also a member of my Soul Group. We've come together in many lifetimes, in all sorts of relationships, to heal this karma. I've paid him back in a few, but more often than not, he's managed to screw me over. He's taken my life work, killed me, and run around on me in a marriage or two. We were on a roll to repeat this pattern once more when we met this lifetime in first a healer/client relationship, and then as teacher/student. But I have finally gotten off the merry–go–round. After several months of working in fear, I confronted this person, told him what I was now doing and that I no longer would be using his modality. He was furious! He accused me of betraying him and plagiarizing his work. I tried to explain that while my work was similar, I was working at an entirely different level. I had taken his work to the next step, not unlike what he did when he developed his modality based on the work of his teacher. He wasn't able to hear anything I said through his pain. I released him in love, refusing to continue the fight. And, after a couple of final encounters, it is now over. It's all about releasing the fear and moving through the situation in love, ending the karmic cycle. Several of my present friends were also with me in this Egyptian incarnation.

They also failed the initiation and died at the hands of this teacher. We came together again as clients and students of this man and bonded. Each of us has individually chosen to end our contracts with him and move forward.

Male, China 370AD

I was in such a foul mood. Nothing I did was working right – certainly nothing anybody else did either! My knee was hurting again and I really felt like I was about to crawl out of my skin. Larry walked in after a hard day at work and I struck out at him, biting with my words. I stormed upstairs, leaving the dinner half–cooked, because I knew I had to do a session on myself before I hurt one or the other of us.

In 370AD, I lived in China. I was a religious leader, quite full of myself, oh so pious. It is not clear exactly what I did to my group of followers, but the ramification of it was that I blocked their spiritual growth in some way. The karma set up by this was a religious archetypal force blocking me from achieving my full potential in this life. I judged this group of individuals (in this life they are my mother and father, my first husband, my niece, my Aunt Lil and probably others that didn't come up in the session) as not being "good enough" to attain higher spiritual consciousness. In order to accomplish this I must have shut down my inner guidance, and I certainly could not have been operating from surrender!

Female, Japan, 800BC

This incarnation was stimulated for me by feelings of rejection. I was going through relationship issues with Larry, primarily created by my own fertile imagination and the influence of this past life being, who was sabotaging my inner clarity. Because my goal was to be happily married, when we would go through periods of unhappiness, I would begin to feel like a failure. I would begin to imagine that Larry was rejecting me for one reason or another. What I found was that in this Japanese lifetime, Larry was my father. At some point, probably when I was a young woman, he sold me to another (my brother, Jake this time around) for material gain. My Inner was holding on to this girl's old belief that there "was nothing I could do to change things." These compressed feelings and emotions have stayed in my field causing anger and fear until I was able to clear them in this session.

The truth was that I was in violation of a Universal Law by not listening to my own inner guidance and trusting in God's Divine Plan for my life. This poor girl that was my soul was too stuck in the rejection and loss to move freely into her future and see the "big picture" of her life. Once again, the original fear of separation acts as a primal force, setting the scene for sadness and failure.

Female, Russia, About 700 AD

About 700 years after the birth of Jesus Christ, I lived as a woman in Russia. During that life I received a very painful and traumatic allopathic medical treatment from a woman healer (my mother in my present life.) Whatever happened left me damaged not only physically but mentally, as well. Go figure – no anesthesia, no antibiotics, no Board Certified physicians… In order to make it through what must have been a dreadful experience, I developed a coping mechanism that left one of my chakras severely damaged. I used blame to help myself make it through this experience, blaming her even though she tried to help me and actually saved my life. The effect that this blaming force has had on my soul is to make it difficult for me to unite in intimacy with others, difficult to give or receive what I really wanted. According to the Universal Laws, what we send out is what returns to us, therefore sending out blame causes others to blame me – thus the karmic cycle is created. This contract continued through into this lifetime. My mother blamed me over and over for not doing or being what she wanted, and I've spent decades blaming her for trying to control me and not letting me be what I wanted to be.

These coping mechanisms, like blaming others or "cursing" others are interesting entities. They are a lot like the genie that Aladdin called forth from the lamp. The genie enabled Aladdin to make it through a difficult crisis. It served a purpose, but Aladdin spent the rest of his life trying to get that entity back into the bottle and out of his life. These coping mechanisms are the same. They definitely serve a purpose during a crisis, but they end up as an ongoing problem. They don't just "block" the chakras of the person that creates them, but actually macerate them. Depending on the level of intensity and emotion surrounding the life crisis – this sort of coping mechanism may actually create an energetic entity in the astral plane.

These entities of sorts live on lifetime after lifetime, generation after generation within a family, creating forces that cause inner pain for the not so lucky recipient and those that are close to them, until they are finally released.

While I have had difficulty with intimacy for most of my life, carrying feelings of being alone and an outcast, the flavor that this example seems to have imparted is a feeling of not being able to be nourished by partnership or association with others. My intentions seem to invert upon themselves: for example, I want to grow my business, but I project a feeling of insecurity, fear or coldness that drives potential clients away from me at a subconscious level. In this particular session, I was able to confront the force, acknowledge the source and clear it, both from the other soul life as well as from my own life! The outcome was a strengthening of my inner purpose, a freedom from worrying about what would happen and an increase in my client base.

Male, Scotland, 840 AD

I found this lifetime when I was doing a session to locate all the fears around generating paying clients and building up my business. What I found was that I was broadcasting out negative energy, like a virus, that was projecting cynicism, coldness and a closed heart. Who would want to come to a healer like that? My power chakra was severely damaged by trauma from this past life, creating a belief that if things get too good, something bad will happen. In this male incarnation, I was financially cruel to others, some of whom were later reincarnated as my daughter Amanda, my husband Larry, his daughter Amy and my ex–husband Graham. I withheld money from them as a form of punishment. I alienated them and basically rejected any form of union we might have had at that time. Since the Universal Law of Cause and Effect says that what we do comes back to us, this force was depriving me of financial inflow and making it very difficult for me to pursue my goals. Not only were clients "rejecting union" with me, but I was really having relationship problems with my stepdaughter. While we've reached an uneasy truce, she still feels pretty much alienated from me to this day.

Female, England, About 870 AD

This session brought up another severely damaged chakra, my power chakra again, which was causing me to be out of alignment with my true identity. It put me in a space where I was manipulating others, trying to make others feel guilty because of my own "suffering," the "everybody hates me" syndrome. What had happened to me in this particular lifetime that set this up in my present incarnation was that I was picked on (by the same souls that re–created this scene when I was in the sixth grade) and made to be ashamed for whom I was and what I did. I began to censor myself via compromise rather than to chance being negatively judged. What a realization! I've done this to myself in this present life since I was a child, constantly being worried about what others might think, to the point that I have not allowed myself to explore all possibilities. This was another contributor to my issues with honesty, both with my self and with others. Most currently, I have experienced criticism (picked on) about my choice to leave the corporate world and make healing my full–time profession. This has manifested in my being taken less than seriously for this choice – for example, it has only been recently that my husband has stopped suggesting, "I get a real job." It seems that only when I began to remove self–imposed restrictions have I been able to stand tall, take responsibility for my destiny and begin the process of self–actualization. I have avoided confrontation over and over throughout this life, denying my authority and my truth rather than standing up and fighting for what I believe. This has only served to prolong the pain, for me and everyone around me.

Female, What's Now New Orleans, About 910 AD

In this lifetime, I was involved in some type of religious practice, perhaps as a priestess. I gave away my power to a man, my mate or partner, who was also involved with this religion. This man took my power because he was jealous of my abilities, bringing to mind the Egyptian lifetime. I subjugated myself to him in order to "make him love me," and as a result, I left that lifetime with the mistaken beliefs that there was no such thing as an inner spiritual life, and certainly that I was not worthy of unconditional love.

In my present life this has manifested as a reluctance to claim my spiritual gifts. It set up a fear of not being "right" in my beliefs along with a suppression of my intuitive abilities. At a physical level, until this force was cleared, I experienced terrific pain in my feet, almost crippling me until the root of the problem was uncovered. As you will soon see, I continued to repeat this cycle in several lives, so it took several sessions to fully alleviate the pain. The InnerSpeak process works like peeling back layers of an onion. As each layer is removed, along with the associated force, a new layer is exposed. Sometimes a block is facilitated away in a single session; sometimes it takes several sessions to completely clear away an issue. However, even in cases where multiple sessions are required, some facet is always healed, so life generally improves while the deeper work is taking place. In another related session on that same lifetime, I uncovered that I was holding the belief that

"I am not powerful." This invalid belief was in direct violation of the Universal Law of No Judgments, which says that we are not to judge others or ourselves, just as God does not judge us. This judgment of myself in that lifetime was causing me to only see examples of love being conditional in my present life. I allowed myself to slip into depression, while rejecting the partnership with my husband. Only when I have been able to claim my power, have I been able to let go of those feelings of not being good enough. (Thank goodness Larry has been very patient with me, and the truth is that he has ALWAYS loved me unconditionally, whether I was able to see it or not!)

Female, Western England, About 950 AD

I seem to have returned to the physical plane fairly quickly to deal with matters of spirituality once more. In this particular lifetime, I was involved with the "old religion," a Pagan and a priestess. Rather than surrendering to God, I kept trying to control things. At some point I became overwhelmed with the responsibility and chose to escape by shutting down my ability to listen to God and refusing to surrender to the direction of Spirit. Dissention began to occur between some of the other priestesses and me, and I was forced to leave the group. I re–connected with this group of women when I was in my thirties. I accepted a position as the manager of marketing communications for a major telecom company. I was hired to manage a group of 21 women and reported to two other women. It was the job "from hell."

I walked into a hotbed of dissention and because I wanted to be liked as the outsider, I tried to make everybody happy and not step on any toes. That strategy was doomed from the start. Eventually I left, vowing never to take a job in marketing, nor work for another woman as long as I lived! Certainly I abdicated my mission for that incarnation, part of which was to recover Mystery, the fool in the Tarot, and Spirit, the realization and expression of myself as an extension of God's image in this world. Once again I had violated the Universal Laws of Order (everything happens under Divine Plan) and No Judgments (Spirit does not judge us, therefore we are not to judge ourselves nor others.) I became tangled in self–disgust and lost faith in myself, closing down my love for my soul and its purpose. I also missed a great opportunity for healing with that group of souls this time around, when I left once again in self–disgust and loss my faith in myself!

Female, What's Now Virginia, About 1080 AD

The problems in this life stemmed from patriarchal abuse, which left me fearful and unable to assign my will to God's will. I was afraid of my father (this soul was with me in my present life as my third husband), and because the culture in which I lived believed that God, or the Great Spirit, was male, I apparently transferred the fear of my earthly father and his abuse to my heavenly Father, and I opted to end the abuse by dying at a young age. This seems to be a fairly common pattern! Part of the emotional trauma I incurred with Tom in this life revolved around religion. He wanted to return to the "old" ways of the Episcopal Church, by reverting to an Anglican sect here in Atlanta. I joined him in this but he quickly became involved in a power struggle with the Bishop of this sect, and this struggle actually ended in handcuffs and a legal battle.

By not trusting God to take care of and protect me, this inner wound also shut down my creative abilities stored in the second chakra, and over several lifetimes I have lived in poverty as well as not being able to find equality in sexual relationships. I violated the Law of Responsibility by not accepting responsibility for my part in creating the abuse and The Law of Balance limiting myself to either feast or famine, either passivity or aggressiveness. In recent years, the force that these traumas created has allowed me to manifest financial hardships for myself, and has also left me with a deep–seated fear of expressing myself openly out of fear of incurring the wrath or rejection of others.

Female, Great Britain, 1120AD

It would appear that I popped back fairly quickly once again to work on the issues I left behind in the prior life – worry about God, abundance, and sexual issues. All of a sudden, clients were canceling appointments or just not showing up, and this was really putting a crimp in my budget! I went into session and found this lifetime where I was a nun. Something sexual happened to me, but I was sworn to secrecy, causing my inner world to become disconnected from reality. I felt lost and unclean, and somehow interpreted this to mean that I was not allowed to receive or have. I had hardly finished the session when my phone started ringing! Within a week, I had more than recovered what I had lost due to the cancellations, but more than that, I had healed a part of myself that was preventing me from fully trusting God to supply my needs.

Female, Great Britain, About 1180AD

This lifetime I did something quite creative – something that should have brought me recognition and fortune – only to have it stolen by another, who took the fame and wealth as well. I allowed this to happen, excusing my behavior with the belief that "I can never get what I want anyway." An interesting point about this scenario is that the person who stole my creative work was also the same soul that was my teacher in the Egyptian lifetime and the man to whom I gave up my power in the New Orleans lifetime! I found this incarnation in a session I did on myself to find relief from terrible stomach pains that started just before I was scheduled for a "get–together" at this man's home early in 2002. The primary lesson I was to learn in that year, although I didn't realize it until the end of the year, was discernment – recognizing wolves in sheep's clothing. My Inner was certainly aware that there was a case with this man, but I didn't figure this aspect out for several more months. This example clearly shows how we get caught up in these karmic cycles with our "soul buddies" and play out similar scripts, trying to clear the karmic contracts that were set up so many years ago and incarnations before.

During another session, the same lifetime came up again. In the next facet, I was still working on issues of releasing my drive and dynamism that had been blocked in a previous life. This trauma happened about 1200AD, or about 20 years later, and by this time I was fairly well entrenched, it would seem, into controlling my feelings at any cost, completely stuck in victim mentality. I felt like I had been cursed, but this construct arose out of my own self–sabotage. Obviously, I had not learned about the Universal Law of Cause and Effect.

This book is a product of healing these inner scars. Through the InnerSpeak process, I have been able to restore my self–confidence, drive, and dynamism and re–open my creative chakra.

Female, Sweden, Early 1200's

In another session on creating a client base and receiving abundance, I uncovered this lifetime where I was pressured out of a partnership against my will. One of the main players in this ostracism was the same soul who played similar negative roles in my lives in Egypt, New Orleans and England. This rejection imparted a sense of otherness, causing this woman to feel like an outcast. My connection with both others and God was stripped away by my loneliness, and the impact on my present life was that I almost felt like I was being chained down into failure. My ability to create or make things happen was being weighed down by the resentment carried forward from that past life. This lifetime came up in a session right about the time that I was confronting the reincarnation of the antagonist. Only in my present life, I was the one leaving, and certainly was not being forced out. As far as this man is concerned, he perceived me as the outcast I was when we were together previously!

It was in this session that I was introduced to one of my angels, Nisroc. Nisroc's role is all about helping us to find freedom. He helps us to tear down the walls of self–imposed prisons, exposing them as the illusions they are.

Female, Scotland, Late 1200's

I was a nun this time around, and because of my vows, I was unable to express what was inside on many fronts. My "manager" was a strict Mother Superior, who demanded I behave according to the rules of the order, which meant keeping quiet at all costs.

I apparently had strong sexual desires, which were entirely inappropriate to the situation and this conflicted me also. Because of the vow of poverty I took, I had nothing of my own. I appear to have shut down my access to inner guidance fairly completely, becoming tangled up in self–disgust and loss my faith in others and myself. In this lifetime, I found what appears to be the first indication of major issues of balance, yin versus yang, receptivity versus manifestation, feminine versus masculine. This session revealed that the traumas from this incarnation left my second chakra blocked enough to impact my sexuality, by walling off of my feelings and forbidding myself to have pleasure.

I appear to have left that life with the fixation that sex and pleasure were taboo. The second chakra governs not only sexuality, but creativity and money as well, so when the sexuality area of one's life isn't working, it's a fairly safe guess that problems in the area of creativity and finances are probably there too.

Female, What's Now Islamabad, 1363AD

I was exploring what happens to one's family and other relationships when an initiation or raising of consciousness takes place,
when I brought up this lifetime, where I was the mother of Larry's
soul, this time, my daughter. She was an artist, very talented, and I
was jealous because she was more talented than I was. I betrayed her
by stifling her creativity, maybe even went so far as to take her art
and promote it as my own. Somehow, I was able to justify my actions
in my own mind, denying that I was doing anything wrong. Besides,
I was the mother, anyway. In this life, Larry has felt betrayed as I've
grown in consciousness. When I left the corporate world, he felt like
I'd violated our agreement that I would always work. All the painful
feelings he must have had almost a thousand years ago came up for
him, along with the massive guilt that I was feeling.

Female, Monterey Mexico, 1410AD

Turn about is fair play, so they say. That's definitely how the
Universal Laws work, and it appears it didn't take very long for me
to get my just desserts. I was a clairvoyant in this incarnation and
my mother shut me down, because she thought what I was doing
was Satan's work.

I ran up against the reincarnation of this mother's soul in a social
setting, in a friend who was constantly judging me, and almost
accusing me of wrong doing, before I even had a chance to do it. It
was interesting to me that the next day after I ran this session on
myself, the dynamics between the two of us changed completely. We

get along great now, and our relationship is a healthy one.

Female, China, 1475AD

This time I was a Chinese noble woman. I became pregnant out of wedlock and took measures to abort the child. Deep regret and guilt were the result, as well as a belief that has kept me from using my own power now. Another fixation I carried forward is "you are not allowed to be happy," as a means of punishing myself for my sin.

Male, Egypt, 1580AD

I was sick with the flu when I did this session. Whatever was making me sick wouldn't lift and it really felt more like an energy intrusion than anything else, so I decided to do a session on myself to see what was causing it. I found a man who died from some sort of epidemic or plague that ended his life before he could accomplish his mission. The force from this past life that was up for me was making me want to escape, sleep; to lose touch with my purpose and to just quit. I literally felt so bad, I truly wanted to give up. When the session was over and the forces from that life were cleared, I began to get well almost immediately.

Female, England, About 1690AD

This is quite a different case from the ones previously

described. The session in which it came up was actually about an ancestral force, but the force was set up in a past life when I was my own ancestor. The ancestor was a woman on my mother's side of my family, and the lessons were all about making appropriate choices and loss of hope.

In this incarnation, my sexuality was out of control, the opposite problem from the life I'd just looked at. I was unfaithful to my husband, denied it, but was rejected by him nonetheless. My sense of authority and inner dignity/uprightness was incomplete.

It seems that no matter how hard I tried, I could not find the satisfaction and love I was looking for. This set up a pattern of "looking for love in all the wrong places" and of confusing love and sex, which subsequently let me leave that lifetime feeling that I was inadequate, that I could not have what I wanted and definitely could not be helped! All my hopes and dreams felt like sad illusions as I left this plane, childless, poor, and very lonely. I had unwittingly violated the Laws of Choices and Patterns – by creating destructive patterns of behavior rather than expressing my creativity in positive manners.

Again, the fear of expressing myself openly in relationship to sex was reinforced, setting the stage in my present incarnation for lack of faith in myself, an unrelenting sense of loneliness and feeling like an outcast.

Female, England, 1750AD

In the previous life, the issues revolved around sexuality, a second chakra problem. The second chakra, or sexual chakra, also houses issues with creativity and finances. In fact, the InnerSpeak process looks at all three areas the same. This incarnation was about financial issues, coupled with spiritual lessons. I was lied to by a religious leader and told that I must give all my worldly goods away in order to save my soul. This had been a popular misconception based on the Church's interpretation of scripture to line its pockets. This woman blamed God for her poverty and shut off her inner guidance. As for me, I was in the process of making a series of bad financial choices myself, but the primary way this force was manifesting was a string of client cancellations and no–shows that were having negative impact on my cash flow. Once I was able to clear her energy from mine, the phone started ringing again and my schedule filled right up once more. An interesting sidebar from this session relates to the soul of the religious leader.

We met once again about fifteen years ago. This time around, he was the Rector of the church I attended. We had "issues" from the time I joined his congregation, but this time, rather than allow him to manipulate me again, I chose to move to a different church.

Female, England, 1850

I came back this time to take another look at rejection of union with God and others. Not much information was available in the session, other than I died in a fire and felt abandoned by God. How this force was impacting me was that I was in the process of channeling in the manual for my modality and I hit "writer's block." After the lifetime was cleared, the information began to flow once more.

Lessons are learned in every lifetime. The incarnations where we did what we were supposed to do and learned what we were supposed to learn are not the source of any problems for us this time around. Everything got resolved; nothing was left hanging. Those lives where we left unresolved issues or didn't complete the mission we signed up for are the ones that we need to examine more closely. The time has come for us to clear up all the loose ends. Recess is over! It feels like a window of opportunity has opened, allowing us to choose to release karmic debt. When the choice is made, it feels like the Divine intervenes through the Law of Grace and wipes the slate clean. It's all about making that choice.

Chapter Eleven
The Rewards

Somewhere along the way, I heard someone say something like "every choice has a price and a prize." Much of this story up to this point has been about the price. Now it's time to quantify the prizes.

Jesus said, "I came that you might have life, and have it more abundantly." At almost fifty–five years of age, I have found abundant life. The little girl who only wanted to be loved had to first figure out how much she loved herself. Once I was able to do that, my eyes were opened and I began to see how much I was loved by others. I began to see that I was making a difference in the lives of those around me. This is what was hidden from me until I began to love myself.

When I was able to let go of all the fear that I had carried for so long, and when I also released the forces that were holding me back, I realized how much I had and how far I had come in a relatively short time.

I attended my first "self–help" workshop, the LRT, in 1989. The year before that I started reading *A Course In Miracles*. At that time, I had no comprehension of what was beginning to happen to me, and certainly could not have foretold how wonderful my life would become in less than fifteen years.

Today, I trust God to provide everything I need. Every morning I wake up, give thanks and meditate. I no longer worry about what might happen next week, next month, next year, or in the next five minutes, because I know that it will be what it is supposed to be. It is in God's hands, and it couldn't be in any better place!

My life runs smoothly without the drama of the earlier years. When it doesn't I stop and surrender. I look around to see what I've been thinking so that I can modify my thoughts to create the reality I desire. I am HAPPY! I am happy ALL the time. I no longer relinquish my power to anything or anyone outside myself. Nobody and nothing can sway me from my place of peace and happiness. I see only peace. I see only love. That is all there is. It doesn't get any better than this!

The blessings I have received in this lifetime run the complete gamut. Even before I began to wake up, I was blessed with success in my career. I was led to be in the right place at the right time so that I was never without a means to provide for my children and myself.

I have met some incredible people in this life. Many of them have come in for a purpose and moved on, however, I count myself lucky to have quite a few friends that have stood by me for many years, supporting and being supported as the needs arise.

I have an incredible family! Larry's story is all through these pages, but Rob and Amanda are still creating theirs. Both of my children have grown into remarkable adults in their own right. They are successful and happy and are in great relationships. They each managed this, despite my personal struggles that took place while they were growing up.

One of the areas of my life that has caused me the most concern over the years has been the number of marriages. Recently, as I was reading the Gospel of John and looking at it from a metaphysical standpoint, I came across the Samaritan woman at the well and her encounter with Jesus. I had an epiphany! Metaphysically, all the women in the Bible represent Divine intuition seeking transformation. Men represent action in the outer world. Jesus told her that she had had five husbands, and that the man she was with now was not her husband. In numerology, the number five is about change toward harmony. In this light, her intuition kept looking for an energy that she could relate to in the outer. She was ready to commit to the correct vibration and Jesus recognized this in her, or he wouldn't have called her out. I now see that I was doing exactly the same thing until I finally found a vibration I could resonate with. It no longer serves me to struggle with guilt over being divorced (nor anything else in my past)!

As The Group, channeled by Steve Rother, so aptly puts it, the fifth dimension is now here. We are now creating heaven on earth. As creators, we are now manifesting our thoughts instantaneously. Because of this, it is more important now than ever before, to constantly monitor what we are thinking. Otherwise we have the ability to manifest third dimensional reality, with its inherent duality, rather than the magnificence we deserve and desire.

Chapter Twelve
Opening To Channel

Channeling is our present example of fifth dimensional communication. For thousands of years people have been receiving
messages from Spirit. In the Holy Bible, there are documentations
of prophesy, but there are also admonitions surrounding commu-
nicating with the dead. The end result is that we have become conflicted about spirit communication. Most of the Protestant sects in
the US denounce it as "dangerous." The Catholics are more toler-
ant, due to the writings of their mystical saints. Then the question
arises of where are the messages coming from – good spirits or bad
ones. There are so many frauds out there, too, so how do you know
who to believe?

After a lifetime of wanting to be psychic, imagine my surprise
when I first started receiving messages from Spirit. Messages had
probably been coming to me for years, but I had dismissed them as
my imagination and assumed I was just talking to myself.

The first time I was consciously aware of what was happening
was in the middle of a class I was teaching. There were six students
learning the InnerSpeak process in a weekend seminar. Something
that had become a part of every class I taught was that at the end
of the weekend I would do a session on the group to clear any
forces that might have been brought up during the weekend. I certainly didn't want anyone to leave feeling overwhelmed.

This particular weekend, it turned out that all the students and
I had shared a lifetime in Egypt. I was a ruler of sorts, one of the
students was my consort and the rest of the class consisted of souls
that I had hurt through the abuse of my power. We were each doing

the facilitation, a visualization where we were to find the person that we were in that life and forgive everyone that was associated with the trauma that occurred. I was shown an image of the Great Pyramid at Giza, and I clearly heard these words, "The capstone has now been replaced." In my visualization, I saw a smaller crystal pyramid being centered on top of the larger one. I was aghast! I was afraid to tell the others, because I thought they would think I was nuts. After a while, I did tell them. One of the students, a practicing psychic, said, "Jean! Wow! You just channeled!"

Now, I find that when I allow myself to be quiet, many times I will receive information. Sometimes it is for me, but many times I'm supposed to give it to another. There are days when I will be working away – writing my book, cleaning the house, playing with my dog – when I will begin to hear, "Go meditate." It will start quietly, but if I ignore it, it will become more and more insistent, until I finally do as I am told. Always, there is something important that wants to come in when this happens.

My methodology is very simple. I take a few deep breaths to center myself. Then I see a column of light coming down, surrounding me. I surrender to Spirit and ask that my guides filter anything that comes in so that I only receive information from the Light, from Source. Then I quietly wait. Many times the first thing that will happen will be that I will begin to see vivid colors – purple, violet, rose, green, blue and yellow, undulating across my field of vision. Then I will get a glimpse of something or I'll perhaps "hear" a message. These are not visions that come through my human eyes or sounds that come through my human ears. No, they are a form of "knowing," something I see or hear in my heart chakra.

Channeling is a great exercise for us because it teaches us to use telepathic communication, which will be the tool that we use in the fifth dimension to talk to one another. It is not, however, something that we can force. It's just not a left–brain activity. We receive from Spirit through our right brains, intuitively, and we have to surrender and trust in order for anything to come through.

Chapter Thirteen
Listening to the Angels

I believe everyone can learn to listen to the angels. Angels are all around us. Some angels are available to everyone, but each of us has "personal ones" as well.

One of the first gifts I received as I began to open to my Higher Self was the ability to see and hear angels. The first time it happened took me quite by surprise. I was in session with a client and the therapy that came up for her was to call in an angel to heal her broken heart. I told the client what she needed to do and went over to a nearby chair to wait until she was done. I closed my eyes for a moment of rest, when I was able to see a most wondrous thing. A beautiful angelic being, complete with wings and glowing with a radiant light was bowing over the table where the client was lying, with the wings spread completely over the client. I thought to myself, "No way this is happening!" When the client was done, I asked her about her experience. She said, "Wow! This beautiful angel came and stretched its wings out over me and I felt more love than I've ever felt in my entire life!" Needless to say, from that time on, every time an angel facilitation came up, I was paying attention! And, more and more, the angels began to come. They are now a very important part of the work I do. Rarely does a session finish without the appearance of at least one. Angels do all manner of wonderful things for the clients, from carrying an ancestor into the light; to showing them how to change the way they are looking at something, to physical healing.

As time went on and I became more involved in my own spiritual growth, I began to notice that many of the people I was now hanging around with had some pretty interesting relationships with angels, teachers and guides. Some of my friends were able to hold conversations with theirs, asking questions and getting answers. I was more than a little jealous, because at that time, all I was able to do was see angels working with my clients. One of my friends, Natasha, is able to see angels and spirits quite clearly, in normal day–to–day life, not just in meditation. She mentioned to me that I always had this blonde haired guy "hanging around." I asked her who he was and what he was doing, but she said she had no idea. She said that he seemed to bring other spirits through to watch me, like he was using me as an example to teach others in whatever dimension he was.

Based on that, I called another friend – one that was able to have the conversations I just mentioned. This friend told me that the blonde haired guy was Michael, the Archangel. This blew me away! Why would an archangel be hanging around me? Why couldn't I see him? What did he want? I kept asking these questions in my daily meditations, but I never got the answer I was looking for, and I certainly was never able to see him like Natasha could. It became an obsession for me. I felt "not good enough" because I was blocked from seeing in the way so many of my peers could. Daily, as I struggled to see, I would end up beating myself up because I felt like a failure. I was SO blocked.

One afternoon, I was riding with my brother, returning from a family funeral. I was bored. You know, one of those "are we there yet" times. I looked out of my window. Apparently my brother wasn't driving fast enough on the four–lane highway, because a big, red transfer truck was passing us on the right. Imagine my surprise when I noticed a large painting on the side of the truck, right behind the driver's door. It was the Archangel Michael holding his big sword and a caption that read, "Archangel Michael, protect our drivers." Even I could see him there! What a great sense of humor they have!

While I still don't see them clearly, I always know they are present – and they are always present. Angels operate under the Universal Law of Non–Intervention. They watch and wait patiently until we ask for their help, but generally don't get involved unless we do ask. Then, they joyfully assist us for our highest and best good.

There has been an occasion or two where my angels have shown up and chastised me. One was described earlier, where I got my hands slapped for having a client re–write the Akashic records. Another happened after a session where I was given a symbol to assist in my healing work. I had asked in the session for help in removing all obstacles, to be able to go to the fifth dimension to work and manifest what is for my highest and best good more quickly. The Archangel Metatron and the Ascended Master Djwhal Khul showed me a symbol to help not only me, but also others to achieve that fifth dimensional state more easily. At the end of every session, I always question how long the processing time will be, and in this case I would be processing the session for nine days. I asked my teachers about the symbol and was told not to use it for myself until I was through with the processing.

In the meantime, the facilitation kept coming up for clients that I should use the symbol to help them go to the fifth and look at their records or build a hologram of what they wanted to manifest in their life. Some fairly incredible stuff was happening in these sessions and I was anxious to try it for myself! After about six or seven days, I couldn't stand it any longer. As I began my morning meditation, I drew the symbol on my forehead and asked to be assisted to the fifth so that I could look at my own Akashic records. Immediately I saw Metatron standing in from of me wagging his finger at me. Busted! He said. "Jean, we told you to wait!" So, wait I did – I mind fairly well. The ninth day finally got there and I started the meditation I'd begun on Wednesday. Nothing happened – NOTHING! I waited and waited, but nothing; no colors, no presences, nothing. I gave up, got dressed and started off to do my errands for the day. I was driving, about a mile from the house, when I heard that familiar voice in my head. "We're sorry you were disappointed this morning, but you shouldn't have been so attached to an outcome. There is no need for you to look at your Akashic records at this time. You are living what is written in the book. You are doing what you are supposed to be doing!" I was so moved that I had to pull my car over and let the tears of joy flow.

The consistent message that I always receive from the angels is that we are so loved. Each and every one of us is adored, more than we could possibly imagine. We each have scores of celestial beings watching over us at all times, holding the Light and creating the space for us to achieve our potential. Take a moment now. Take a few deep breaths and relax. Feel the love that surrounds you. Feel the brush of a wing on your cheek. Smell the light scent of roses in the air. Know you are loved!

Chapter Fourteen
The Ascended Masters

In addition to angels, there are a whole host of celestial beings that are standing by to help us. They wait patiently until we are ready and ask for their assistance. They work with us primarily as teachers and guides. The majority of my experience, besides angels, has been with Ascended Masters. Angels are a species unto themselves. They are not, nor have they ever been, human. Ascended Masters, on the other hand have had at least one incarnation on the earth plane. They have reached the pinnacle where it is the choice of their soul not to return to human form, but to remain available to assist us.

Probably the best known Ascended Master is the one known to us as Jesus. He is the Son of God who took human form to bring Light back to the planet. He came as the bridge for mankind. He came to teach us how to live in concert with the Universal Laws and how to live in harmony with the Mosaic Laws, the laws of man. He came to show us that we are the masters of matter. His example was the ability to ascend, to heal the sick, to teleport, to manifest, and to raise the dead. What we didn't get told in church was that he was born into a very special family, and that his parents, Joseph and Mary are also Ascended Masters. They were Essenes, members of an orthodox Jewish sect that lived apart from others, who went within and spoke with God. They were priests by their own right.

Djwhal Khul, the Tibetan, is another Master who has had a profound influence on my life. It was he that woke me up in the middle of the night and began to fill my field with Sacred Geometry. It was he that came to me and blessed me with the Universal Symbol, a tool to assist others in their ascension process. And, it is he that frequents my meditations to keep me on this path.

The Ascended Masters Quan Yin and Lady Nada are two of the other female teachers who work with us. Quan Yin is of Tibetan origin, and is the Master of Compassion. Lady Nada assists with healing through her Pink Flame. She brings reassurance and discernment to those on their Spiritual Path. Master Kuthumi had incarnations as Pythagorus and St Francis of Assisi. He brings illumination, education and wisdom through love. He has an incredible sense of humor and has been extremely patient with me in my struggles toward enlightenment.

Master St. Germain is the Master of the Violet Flame. In one lifetime he was Merlin. He burns away all that is not true with his flame. Master Sai Baba is actually in physical form at this time in India, however he is omnipresent and appears around the world, helping us learn important lessons about Unconditional Love.

El Morya incarnated as the wise man Melchior, as King Arthur and more recently as St. Thomas More. The Master Hilaron was once St. Paul. Others who work with me are Gautama Buddha and Serapis Bey, but these are merely a few of the Ascended Masters.

As you begin to grow spiritually and ask for enlightenment, discernment and wisdom, they will come to you. For many of us who are still "asleep" they work with us in our dream state. For those who practice meditation, they readily come when the mind is quiet. In the beginning, I saw them only as color – St. Germain was violet, of course, Djwhal Khul is deep purple, Sai Baba appears orange, and Kuthumi is a speckled blend of lime green and turquoise. More recently, as I have opened myself more fully, I have begun to see them more clearly. From time to time Djwhal Khul will appear as a complete figure in purple robes. I only ever see Lady Nada's eyes, or the outline of Sai Baba's gigantic afro, but I am seeing more and more as time goes on.

Chapter Fifteen
Finding Your Purpose

No one (either on the physical plane or in Spirit) can tell you why you are here. Your Mission is something that you have to figure out for yourself. Of one thing you can be sure, you are here to express some facet of God through your existence. We are each an individuated part of All That Is, created in the image of Father/Mother God. So, each of our purposes on this earth we call home is to display some aspect of the Divine in our lives. Since God is All That Is, there are several aspects of the Divine that have come up in my work with clients that I will attempt to share with you. It seems that whatever aspect of our particular purpose will be a part of our life that we have had continual struggle with. Remember, we are here to heal the pain of our soul that has been created through incarnation after incarnation where we violated Universal laws.

Some of our souls come in to demonstrate Unconditional Love. Many times those with this Mission struggle with issues of hatred, fear, and rejection before they finally break through their forces enough to be able to experience true freedom and understanding of their purpose. Others have a Mission of Mystery (this is one of mine). Those working through the mystery in their lives tend to start off as control freaks, until one day they are clear enough to step off into the void, trusting in the wings of Spirit to protect and guide them as they demonstrate to those in their lives the joy of the Unknown.

Another Mission is that of Evolving, spiritual growth throughout their life that leads to the understanding of the greater powers that be. The other side of this is the Mission of Dharma, the path of spiritual duty. Both of these variations have the same goal – finding Heaven in one's earthly home.

The Mission of Beauty is an interesting one. Gifted artists are often here to work this purpose, but surprisingly enough it also comes up for people that incarnate with a seeming disfigurement or disability. Many people come in with Manifesting as their purpose – learning to receive what one creates, realizing that we are in fact co–creators of our own reality and that we are here to understand that we are the masters of matter – not the other way around. A biggie for some souls is Honor – dedicating one's incarnation to dealing with integrity, dignity and power issues.

It might seem that having the Mission of Play would be the purpose of choice – until we remember that our soul purpose is generally a big struggle for us. This means that working Play probably means having to overcome Not Play (workaholics that don't think they deserve to have fun for whatever reason.) What about Transmuting as a soul job? These are usually the folks who just can't tolerate change, motion and transformation. Souls working Friendship generally struggle with intimacy, companionship and passion. Hearing shows up more often that one might expect. This Mission is about receiving guidance from one's Higher Self, hearing the still, small voice of God. Fear, anger, low self–esteem, lack of trust – all cause us to turn a deaf ear to the truth that is there to teach, love and guide us on our path. An aspect of my Mission that I only recently found is Definition, learning to define my boundaries and those of others.

These are just a few. Perhaps you have resonated with one that I've mentioned. It doesn't matter. You wouldn't have picked this book up if you were not at least moving toward the path that you chose before you came into this lifetime. As a clue, take a long look at the areas of your life that have been a particular and repetitive problem for you. This will shed light on what may be why you are here.

None of us has a true conception of how our lives and our Mission actually affects those we come in contact with. A seemingly inconsequential encounter can have a profound effect on another person – sometimes positive, sometimes negative. But, when we are walking our path, working our soul's Mission, these encounters will be informative and uplifting – an inspiration to those that need to see what you are displaying. This is how we are each able to demonstrate what God is.

There is an old science called numerology that can also be effective in helping you to understand why you are here. First you will need to determine your birth number. This is fairly simple:

1. Write your birth date out, mm/dd/yyyy.

2. Trade out the "slashes" for "plus signs" (+).

3. Add all the digits to get a sum.

4. If the sum is a two–digit number, add those two digits to get a final sum.

Here are brief descriptions of soul purposes based on birth number. Those souls working One are here to learn about creativity and confidence. Two's are all about cooperation and balance. Three's work on emotional expression and sensitivity. Four's are all about stability and process.

The souls working Five are here to learn about freedom, discipline and change. Six's are all about self–acceptance. Seven's are about trust, love and the outdoors. Folks like myself working Eight are learning about money and power (feast or famine in my case)! Nine's are dealing with integrity. And Ten's (zero) come in with inner gifts, like intuition, and have to learn to bring them to fruition. There have been many volumes written about numerology that will provide you with more information.

This is a baseline to help begin this exploration process to find the answers that only you can find. My goal is to whet your appetite and to encourage you on your path!

Chapter Sixteen
Clearing The Path To Higher Consciousness & Ascension

The consciousness–raising that began in the late sixties and took on greater proportions with the arrival of the Indigo Children in the eighties and nineties is affecting most of us now in some way and degree. These kids began being born to change the world. They come already remembering who they are and what they are here to do. Guilt is not part of their make–up, and this has created a rough road for many of them, but they have begun the process of waking us all up. Many of us are beginning to focus our thoughts on enlightenment, ascension and getting in touch with our own Divinity, whether we use those terms or not.

There appear to be very similar signals that we are experiencing as we move down this path. Are you finding yourself waking up in the middle of the night or having very intense dreams? Have you been thrust into a change in career or job, perhaps unexpectedly? Are you experiencing aches and pains, particularly in the neck and back, which you never felt before? Are you feeling sad or lonely, like you just don't "fit in" with your old relationships and family? How about "hearing things" inside your head and feeling ungrounded? If any of these ring true for you, you are on the right path, the one that leads upward from old third dimensional thought patterns and to the higher consciousness of the fourth and fifth dimensions!

At this time, changes are occurring to us physically, as well.

The new consciousness begins the opening process of a new chakra, the one I call High Heart or Christ Consciousness. The physical location of this chakra is between the heart and the throat, and the organ related to it is the thymus. The function of this new chakra is to awaken us to Universal Love and the expression of it in each of our lives. A second new chakra is beginning to open, as well. I call it the Ascension chakra, and it is located directly opposite the mouth at the occiput on the back of the head. Additionally, our bodies are crying out for the reawakening of additional strands of DNA, ones that have not been used for thousands of years. Awakening your DNA strands creates a dialog between your higher consciousness and your physical body, anchoring into your physical energy the divine wisdom of your higher self. Activating these new DNA strands begins the process of direct communication between your physical DNA and Spiritual DNA (your higher consciousness) and this centers your own divine wisdom within your being and your consciousness.

Activating your DNA creates a magnet for those things your higher self is manifesting, in all areas of your life. The third component of movement on this path is the letting go of those things that are holding us back in lower realms of thought – fears, judgment, forces and attachments to people and things. Many of us have spent much time and money working to clear "issues" that we have created during this lifetime, but these make up only a small part of the forces that hold us back. These "issues" and forces are also what propel us forward, to begin the process of waking up. Now is our opportunity to release and clear old karmic contracts, once and for all. It's also our time to heal old ancestral pain that we have inherited. Most importantly, though, we are now free to release ourselves from duality, where we've always felt the need to judge everything as "bad" or "good," "wrong" or "right" and where we've felt separate from others and Spirit. The two greatest roadblocks on our path to higher levels of consciousness are fear and judgment. As long as these remain, our progress is limited. The message for all of us now is that everything just "is", and our place is not to judge anything or anyone any further than that. When we are able to see the Divinity in others, we can release any need for attachments. Sound easy? If we could learn to assign our will to Spirit and walk in surrender all day, every day, we would have no forces, no pain. We would be blessed with all the abundance, health, happiness and love that we deserve – that is ours by Divine right. Unfortunately, we are human and we have our "mortal moments." We must learn to discern when we are operating from our earthly self rather than our higher self, so that we can plan our actions accordingly. When we are operating from surrender, working our plan from our higher self, everything flows. Not only does life feel good for us, but also those around us receive the light that we emit and they benefit as well. When our choices are God's choices, they WORK. Stress does not exist within our higher selves. When we operate from our earthly self, our energies are scattered. It becomes difficult to find our way. Struggle enters into the equation. Most of the time we don't recognize that we have slipped into one of these "mortal moments".

A priority for each of us needs to be discernment – the ability to recognize when we are operating in surrender and when we are not. The second priority is that when we find we are working from our earthly self, we should MAKE NO DECISIONS! This is an imperative that will prevent us from making those mistakes that are harmful for both those around us and ourselves. We don't violate Universal Laws when we are in a state of surrender – only during "mortal moments." We also don't create those attachments that then become obstacles on our path to Ascension.

Actually there are tools that are readily available to each of us to assist in this process. My work, InnerSpeak, opens up your ability to communicate with your "Inner Essence" or Soul to find the past life or ancestral traumas that need to be healed in order to end karmic cycles. It was through this process that the material you've read so far was found, as I began my own time of "waking up." DNA activations in several forms are available to support opening your creativity and intuition, as well as beginning the process of physical healing and change in your bodies. Meditation provides a path for us to go within and find many of our answers there.

Whichever modality appeals to you, now is the time to begin that process of "letting go". We are very supported. Our Angels, Teachers, Guides and the Ascended Masters are waiting for each of us to "wake up". They work with us constantly, whether we are aware of their presence or not, but since we operate in a world of free will, they generally don't intervene in our lives unless we invite them too. All you have to do is ask!

We live in a world of choices. We are so blessed that we can choose where, how, when and why we live. We can choose to awaken to our destiny at any point in our life. We can choose how we wish to react to anything that presents itself on our path, and it is our choice whether we want to judge or not. Moment by moment we make our choices and create our lives. We can choose to see peace or turmoil, love or fear. The time is NOW – Choose with awareness!

Appendix
Typical InnerSpeak Files

1:1 SPIRITUAL

1:2 RETURN

1:3 GAIA

1:4 CREATION

1:5 SOUL STAR

1:6 EJECTION

1:7 MOVE

1:8 CLARITY

1:9 STRENGTH

2:1 DATABANK

2:2 JUSTICE

2:3 LIGHTHOUSE

2:4 DEATH

2:5 TEMPERANCE

2:6 DEVIL

2:7 SOUL REACTION

2:8 EMOTIONAL

2:9 CAUSAL EVENT

3:1 PASSAGE

3:2 MISSION

3:3 REALIGNMENT

3:4 MEANING

3:5 BLADDER MERIDIAN
3:6 GALL BLADDER MERIDIAN
3:7 HEART MERIDIAN
3:8 KIDNEY MERIDIAN
3:9 LARGE INTESTINE MERIDIAN

4:1 LIVER MERIDIAN
4:2 LUNG MERIDIAN
4:3 SEX/CIRCULATION MERIDIAN
4:4 SMALL INTESTINE MERIDIAN
4:5 SPLEEN MERIDIAN
4:6 STOMACH MERIDIAN
4:7 TRIPLE WARMER MERIDIAN
4:8 CONCEPTION VESSEL MERIDIAN
4:9 GOVERNING VESSEL MERIDIAN

Source

The origination of the force at hand.

1:1 Plan B Contract – choice of parents changed just prior to incarnation

1:2 This Lifetime

1:3 Early childhood trauma/abuse.

1:4 Force set up during the conception, gestation process

1:5 Birth Trauma

1:6 Force from mother during labor or at the birth moment

1:7 Paradigm Shift

1:8 Self Sabotage as a way to avoid transformation

1:9 During Incarnation Process

2:1 Ancestor – locate lineage and how many generations back

2:2 Ancestral Other Life

2:3 Reincarnated Ancestor

2:4 Lost Ancestor – either aborted or "hiding"

2:5 Ancestor that had no children to clear for them

2:6 From both ancestral lines

2:7 Own ancestral force resonates with ancestral force of partner

2:8 Twin conceived at same time that didn't reach viability

2:9 Deep Ancestry – more than 16 generations ago

3:1 Past Life

3:2 One was one's own ancestor

3:3 Past Life Ancestral

3:4 Past Life Partner's Force

3:5 Future Life

3:6 Future Life Soul Group

3:7 Alien Influence

3:8 Psychic Attack

3:9 Leak – one is trying to delay this force

4:1 Veil of Death – person wants help or closure

4:2 Partner's Force and you resonate with it

4:3 Death during birth of mother or child.

4:4 Soul Group Member

4:5 Attachment – Parasitic presence or entity.

4:6 Cultural, family or religious implant

4:7 CURSE– Evil intent returns to its source.

4:8 Authority figure overwhelms one.

4:9 Won't Regress

Causal Event

A crisis that has caused the inner to reorganize itself in a negative way, due to the memories of these wounds.

1:1 Broken heart

1:2 Bigamy or adultery

1:3 Deformed (physically or inwardly), physical maiming or illness

1:4 Expulsion, pushed out, ostracized, abandonment

1:5 Suppression of financial, sexual or creative abundance

1:6 Forced into or out of a partnership (usually by family or cultural pressure)

1:7 Abortion, infanticide, fetal or seed idea not allowed to reach viability, rejected child or goal, miscarriage, lost child

1:8 Birth death – check mother or child

1:9 Amputation, cutting the umbilical cord, physical or emotional disconnection

2:1 Financial or sexual cruelty

2:2 Loss of heart, shame or bitterness from being excluded from family or group

2:3 "Sin"

2:4 Arranged or no love marriage

2:5 Sexual enslavement, jealousy, or other situation or problem

2:6 Servitude, powerless before the will of others

2:7 Sudden betrayal

2:8 Punishment for another's misdeeds

2:9 Concealment of homosexuality or of a homosexual act

3:1 Deception – others don't know who or what one really is or what one is really doing

3:2 Impotence or frigidity, not wanting sex, financial failure

3:3 Incest, molestation, forced sodomy or rape

3:4 Renouncing faith in God

3:5 Loss of faith in self or others

3:6 Deep suppression of inner expression (self or other)

3:7 Early childhood abuse

3:8 Failure, ruin, impoverishment

3:9 Attempted suicide

4:1 Torture (physically or emotionally overwhelmed)

4:2 Unable to provide for loved ones, or perceived endangerment of family

4:3 Child or other loved one taken away

4:4 Natural disaster or accident that results in death

4:5 Abuse of power that causes hurt to self or another

4:6 Stuck walking a path that one knows is not right for oneself

4:7 Revenge or illness as revenge

4:8 Denied infidelity

4:9 Betrayal, treachery, being lied to or lying

Renewal

Facilitations to replace the removed forces with positive intentions

1:1 TL on the body for an open door to the force. Close the door.

1:2 Ask the ancestor or other life being to show what's in their heart.

1:3 Walk hand–in–hand with the ancestor/being into transforming fire.

1:4 Create a bottle. Invite the being into it. Cork and give to God.

1:5 Open self fully to the Grace of God & ask that peace be restored

1:6 Send love to ancestor / past life being.

1:7 Ask an Angel to enfold self, ancestor or being until the force lifts.

1:8 Support the ancestor or other life being in confronting the force

1:9 Acupuncture to help one unfold past an old inner wound.

2:1 Bless the TL with an oil

2:2 Ask God to remove the mirrors in one's field.

2:3 Allow one's Divine Right of abundance to be re–integrated

2:4 Fill vessel with light and allow it to be seen by the world

2:5 Change the vibration of the body to jumpstart a rebirthing process.

2:6 Pray to recover a sense of self worth and value.

2:7 Ask God to remove the black fountains in the field

2:8 Find the ancestor. Ask them to show you the scene where they are.

2:9 Remove the energy of the person/attacker/ancestor from all cells

3:1 Ask God to remove the creature or monster in the TL.

3:2 Move the feeling from the TL to the heart and let it be trans-muted

3:3 Allow the other life being to vent their rage or fear until it's gone.

3:4 Go to the other life scenario & collect the gifts/tools that were left.

3:5 Place a crystal on the force TL.

3:6 "Divine Connection"

3:7 Help the ancestor or other life being mourn by attending their own funeral to end the cycle on this force.

3:8 Confront the "source" in love and affirm the contract is complete.

3:9 TL for two points and hold until polarity is felt.

4:1 Worship God together with the ancestor or other life being.

4:2 Find the question that needs to be answered.

4:3 Dance with the ancestor or other life being.

4:4 Have self, ancestor or other life being take responsibility for this force and release it to God.

4:5 Allow client to move to the 5th to view Akashic Records and/or create hologram of perfect solution

4:6 Call in one's Soul Group to assist.

4:7 Find the "faces" in one's field and ask God to take them to the light.

4:8 Take down the enclosure or trap that the ancestor or other life being is trapped in. It's usually a belief or a fixation, so check the Belief or Fixations file first.

4:9 Visualize a star in the 5th. Wrap your DNA strands around the star & pull the star's energy into yourself through your DNA

Universal Laws

When we ignore or reject one of the Universal Laws, we set in motion a force or karmic debt that must be cleared at some point in the path of the Soul. These are just a few of the most important ones. – (A) Automatic laws, they happen whether we choose them or not.

Law of Action – action is required to bring thought, feeling or knowledge to life.

Law of Identity (A) – all experiences and things in our lives are seeking to teach us who we really are.

Law of Attraction (A) – basic law of manifestation, where the attention is, that is what will be created, whatever the mind believes intensely will come to pass.

Law of Balance (A) – the Universe will immediately counterbalance any impact so that life can be maintained and supported lovingly (as one door closes another opens…).

Law of Cause and Effect – principle of Karma. Everything happens according to law – whatever you do returns back to you at some point.

Law of Right To Decree – this law allows the ascended realms to intervene in our behalf. Always add "under the law of Grace" to your decree. Repeat 3 times, adding "It is done, It is done, It is done. I thank you" and let it go, trusting it is in higher hands.

Law of Divine Flow – if we live in the moment, centered in love, all flows well.

Law of Economy of Force – adjusts all to the best advantage with the least expenditure of force for the material and spiritual evolution of the Cosmos (if it's easy for me, it's right for me).

Law of Correspondence (A) – as soon as the thought is created, the object is next to it. Every desire or question has its answer right next to it. As soon as there is an energy surge in Divine Mind, the totality of the experience is right there.

Law of the Vacuum (A) – nature abhors a vacuum. Clear a space – like energy returns.

Law of Forgiveness – seeing all with love, good follows.

Law of Free Will – we have the right and power to choose our direction.

Law of Grace – God can waive the Law of Karma in that a person can receive more than one deserves if it is for the good of all.

Law of Group Endeavor – when 2 or 3 are gathered together in my name.

Law of Honesty – only when we are honest with ourselves can we be honest with another.

Law of Intention – energy must follow intention for manifestation to occur.

Law of Magnetic Control – every thought we have creates a match that boomerangs back at us.

Law of No Judgments – Universal Spirit does not judge us. Our judgments attract judgments in equal measure.

Law of Non–Attachment – attachment to the self creates karma. Non–attachment dissolves karma. Through spiritual practice man can free himself from karmically determined existence.

Law of Non–Intervention – it's not our job to intervene or correct what we see as harmful behavior. We are to work in our own reality only otherwise great karma is set.

Law of Order (A) – Everything, if left to its own devices will always be in Divine order.

Law of the Present Moment – time does not exist; the here and now is all we have.

Law of Rhythm (A) – everything flows – in and out, ebb and flow, the pendulum swing manifests in everything. Only in the ebb can energy be redefined to express in a new and higher way.

Law of Giving and Receiving (A) – as we give, so will energy return to us (give freely, receive freely; give cautiously, receive cautiously).

Law of Unconditional Love – loving others and ourselves as they are, honoring our own and the path of all other's souls. It is loving without judgment or reservation.

Law of Vibration – the basis of manifestation, nothing rests, everything moves.

A Guided Meditation

This meditation is designed to assist you in the exploration of the dimensions you live in. It will help you to become acquainted with your angels, teachers and celestial guides. It can be used to explore past and future existences. It is also available on CD, along with other meditations, from the author, Jean Adrienne.

Begin by getting comfortable – either lying down or preferably sitting in a comfortable chair with your feet on the floor. Let you hands rest gently by your sides. Start by closing your eyes and taking a few deep breaths to cleanse and center. Begin breathing normal breaths and focus your attention on the inhale and exhale of each one. Allow yourself to become very relaxed. Ask that a column of white light come down from Source and surround you, keeping you calm and safe. Open your heart and let this beautiful light enter and fill you with warmth. You feel so warm, so relaxed, so comfortable, so loved. Good. Ask your Mother / Father God to raise your vibration now, first to 83 hertz to open your third eye. Good. Now ask that your vibration be raised to 108 hertz, the Point of All Knowing. Excellent! Now, ask that you be lifted up from this third dimensional plane, move through the fourth dimension and into the fifth dimension. Good. Look around you. See how beautiful everything appears in the fifth dimension. There is a violet golden glow that surrounds everything you see. This is the dimension of manifestation. It is the Universal Mind. Everything you desire can be first created here to manifest later in the third dimension. Here you can create a hologram of your heart's desire.

Imagine it to be like a giant snow globe, one that you can actually enter for yourself and walk around inside. Create, now, all the scenarios that you wish to manifest. Take your time and make everything exactly the way you'd like it. Make sure you've included everything, in fact look around, there are two things you've forgotten. Bring them in now. Good. Now close your hologram and offer it up to God. Ask that everything that is yours by Divine Right be given to you now, under Grace, in a Perfect Way. Give thanks! Good. It is done, it is done, it is DONE!

Now, ask that you be lifted to the seventh dimension, the Dimension of Light. Here you are able to see auras, the Lightbodies that surround us. Look around you. Notice the Lights of all those that are near you. Feel the feelings in the Lights.

Now we will be lifted up to the eighth dimension. This is the dimension of Now Into The Past. Here you can view your past lives and the experiences of your soul. In this dimension, you can ask to be shown the aspects that your soul selected to bring in this lifetime. These are aspects from other lifetimes, not only yours, but aspects of other's lives that you chose to work on in this incarnations. Take a moment and explore the first aspect you find. Now, ask this aspect to rotate back and allow another to come forward. Good. Now ask this aspect to rotate back and allow another to come forward. Good. Now ask this aspect to rotate back and allow another to come forward. Excellent. Now ask that you be shown the lifetime that has the most profound influence on you this time around. Look around and see who is with you. See if you can tell what contracts were set up then.

Now let's move upward to the ninth dimension, the dimension of celestial beings. This is the dimension where your angels, teachers and guides exist. Now is the time to meet them. First look toward your right shoulder, where your Joy angel is. Feel her tickle your right cheek or give you a kiss there. Ask her to come front and center so that you can meet her. Ask her to give you her name. Spend a few moments getting to know her. Good. Now, ask her to move back to your right and ask your guide that's in front of you and to your left to step forward. This guide is generally indigenous to your origins. If you are American, it will most likely be a Native American. Ask his/her name. Take a moment to get acquainted. Good. Ask if there is any information that he/she has for you at this time. Excellent.

Now ask that the Archangel Michael be present with you. Thank you. Feel the love he has for you as you bask in the blue glow that emanates from his presence. Archangel Michael, I ask that you assist me in clearing old attachments and the cords that connect me to the past. These old cords and attachments no longer serve me. They drain the energy, not only from me, but from those that have attached to me as well. Notice now as the Archangel Michael stands in front of you with his blue sword. He cuts all the cords that have been attached to the front and the sides of your bodies. All old energy is now sent back to its source in love. Now the Archangel Michael stands behind you, cutting all the cords that have been attached over time to your back, sending all that energy back to the source. Thank you, Archangel Michael for this wonderful gift of love.

Now it is time to return to the here and now, back into your body, back into the physical plane. As you return down through the dimensions, give thanks and bid farewell for now to all those that you have met today. Gently let yourself come into the present. Feel the chair underneath you. Wiggle your fingers and toes. Take a deep breath, and as you exhale it from your heart, give thanks to Spirit for this wonderful experience. When you are ready, you may open your eyes.

About the Author

Jean Adrienne Bevil, is a healer, teacher, lecturer and creator of quantum change. She is a graduate of The Florida State University with a BA in Psychology. She also completed the four–year Education For Ministry program from The University of the South's Episcopal Seminary. She developed the InnerSpeak Process and is also a Usui Reiki Master, Karuna Ki Master and Seven Rays Master. She offers healing sessions in her home in Roswell, Georgia, where she lives with her husband, Larry and their dog, Crissy. Together, she and Larry have three grown children, Rob Trott, Amanda Trott and Amy Peddie.

The InnerSpeak Process can also be used as an excellent remote healing tool. The session is done based on your information and photo, and the session report is either mailed or e–mailed upon completion. Jean Adrienne may be contacted for sessions via jeanadrienne@mindspring.com. More information on the Process is available at www.inner–speak.com.

Mardeene B. Mitchell is a writer, writing coach, publishing consultant, speaker, book developer, and collaborator on a selective basis. Her mission is to bring visionaries and visionary ideas to light to facilitate personal and global transformation. She was collaborative writer with Dr. Sheldon Z. Kramer, Ph.D. on Hidden Faces of the Soul: 10 Secrets for Mind/Body Healing from Kabbalah's Lost Tree of Life, endorsed by Deepak Chopra, M.D. (Adams Media Corporation, Boston, 2000), and with Dr. Jill Kahn, *The Gift of Taking: Honor Yourself First... All Else Will Follow*, 2001.

She is based in the metro Atlanta, Georgia, area. mardeene@mind-spring.com

Soul Adventures Quick Order Form

Telephone Orders: (404) 934–0714; have credit card ready

Email Orders: jeanadrienne@mindspring.com

Postal Orders: Jean Adrienne,
690 Wexford Hollow Run, Roswell, GA 30075, USA.

Please send a copy of Soul Adventures ___ $16.95 US.

Please send more FREE information on:
__ Speaking / Seminars__ InnerSpeak Sessions __ Mailing List

Name:_____

Address:_____

City:_____State:_____Zip:_____

Telephone:_____

Email Address:_____

Sales Tax: Please add 7% for books shipped to Georgia

Shipping:
US: $4.00 for the first book, $2.00 for each additional book
International: $9.00 for the first book; $5.00 for each additional book

Payment: Check___ Credit Card____ (Visa or Mastercard)

Card Number:_____
Exp. Date_____

Name on card:_____